free &
løcked up!

free & løcked up!

Essays Delivered at the
Lutheran Study Days 2020 Conference
in Bergen, Norway 60.3913° N, 5.3221° E

Edited by
John W. Hoyum

FIFTEEN-SEVENTEEN PUBLISHING · 1517.

Published by:
1517 Publishing
PO Box 54032
Irvine, CA 92619-4032

Publisher's Cataloging-In-Publication Data
(Prepared by Cassidy Cataloguing Services)

Names: Lutheran Study Days (Conference) (2020 : Bergen, Norway) | Hoyum, John W., editor.
Title: Free and locked up! : essays delivered at the Lutheran Study Days 2020 Conference in Bergen, Norway / edited by John W. Hoyum.
Description: Irvine, CA : 1517 Publishing, [2022] | Includes bibliographical references.
Identifiers: ISBN: 978-1-956658-24-8 (hardcover) | 978-1-956658-25-5 (paperback) | 978-1-956658-26-2 (ebook)
Subjects: LCSH: Liberty—Religious aspects—Lutheran Church—Congresses. | Christian life—Lutheran authors—Congresses. | LCGFT: Conference papers and proceedings. | Essays. | BISAC: RELIGION / Essays. | RELIGION / Christianity / Lutheran. | RELIGION / Christian Theology / General.
Classification: LCC: BT810.3 .L88 2022 | DDC: 233.7—dc23

Printed in the United States of America.
Cover art by Zacharaiah James Stuef

Table of contents

Introduction

John W. Hoyum

The theme of freedom is one of the signal features of Luther's Reformation. This might initially strike some as strange for a figure in whom we find a profound attack on human freedom, specifically in the form of free will. Luther's rejection of natural human capacity for free choice is argued most famously in *The Bondage of the Will* (1525). Alongside this argument, Luther asserts the freedom of God in election delivered through the gospel proclaimed in preaching, attached to baptismal water, and joined to the elements of bread and wine in the Lord's Supper. Only in God's word do we find God's free choice for us, a choice secured by the death and resurrection of Jesus Christ. And yet it is also—strangely enough—where Christians discover what freedom truly means. Christian freedom is first of all freedom from the powers of sin, death, the devil, and law. It is also freedom from the sinful human quest to seek God rather than be found by him. What the gospel promises is a dangerous kind of freedom that appears to go too far, neglecting the tasks and limitations of creaturely life in a world still marked by sin.

And yet the Lutheran Reformation has much to say about what freedom really is in such a situation. The essays collected here venture some answers as to what Christian freedom means for justified sinners alive in Christ, dead to the old sinful self, and tasked with a vocation to an old and dying world populated by fellow sinners. It is fitting that these essays were originally delivered as lectures during the summer of 2020 in Bergen, Norway, for the annual Lutheran Study Days conference. That year marked 500 years since the publication

of Luther's *The Freedom of a Christian*—one of the pioneering treatises of the reformer's career. For Luther, the Christian is free and
subjected to nothing, and yet, at the same time, subject in servitude to
the neighbor. It is this subjection to the neighbor that forms the basis
for Luther's frequently overlooked doctrine of vocation. It is to this
twofold freedom and servitude that these essays devote themselves.

The conference was held virtually in the early months of the
novel coronavirus pandemic that kept many people away from home,
work, school, and church. It was therefore a fitting occasion to pause
over the question of Christian freedom, especially since the various
arenas of human social life were on hiatus with the world on lockdown. Freedom, that summer, seemed elusive. Normally, Lutheran
Study Days would be a time of gathering and conversation around
food and drink, with a concluding Sunday morning worship service.
It would usually be a time for reuniting with old friends and making
new ones. But in 2020, the conference was held online by necessity.
And the world's situation proved timely for these reflections on freedom because, for Luther, Christian freedom is not something lived in
solitude. The fabric of human life with all its various relationships and
responsibilities—family, civil society, the church, and the state—is
the context in which those who are free in Christ exercise their many
and various callings.

To expand and celebrate the effort of the Lutheran Study Days
conference to get this material into the hands of as many people as
possible, 1517 has coordinated with the event organizers to bring the
most impactful lectures together in one edited volume. We are very
thankful that they have partnered with us to disseminate the valuable
work you find within these pages.

Freed to Be Holy[1]

Robert Kolb

Luther's *Large Catechism* informs readers who the Holy Spirit is by telling what kind of goal his actions have, and what they accomplish. He writes, "As the Father is called a Creator and the Son is called a Redeemer, so on account of what he does the Holy Spirit must be called a Sanctifier, or one who makes us holy." Luther continues, "Just as the Son obtains lordship by taking possession of us through his birth, death, and resurrection, etc., so the Holy Spirit effects our being made holy through the following: the community of saints or Christian church, the forgiveness of sins, the resurrection of the body, and the life everlasting." Luther observed that Christ's sufferings, death, and resurrection would have remained hidden from us, apart from the Holy Spirit's sanctifying work: "it would have been all in vain, all lost. In order that the treasure might not remain buried but be put to use and enjoyed, God has caused the Word to be published and proclaimed, in which he has given the Holy Spirit to offer and apply to us this treasure, this breaking of what bound us."[2]

---

[1] This essay reflects the work brought together in my *Luther's Treatise on Christian Freedom and Its Legacy* (Lanham, MD: Fortress Academic/Lexington, 2019) and my translation of the German *The Freedom of a Christian* (Wheaton: Crossway, 2021).

[2] *Die Bekenntnisschriften der Evangelisch-Lutherischen Kirche*, ed. Irene Dingel (Göttingen: Vandenhoeck & Ruprecht, 2014, [henceforth BSELK]) 1058–1061; *The Book of Concord*, ed. Robert Kolb and Timothy J. Wengert (Minneapolis: Fortress, 2000, [henceforth BC]), 435–436.

For Luther, sanctification was not first of all a description of the kind of life we lead, but it rather defined our experience of what the Holy Spirit does to us and who he is for us. In his *Small Catechism*, his treatment of "sanctification" in the Creed says only that we cannot by our own understanding or strength believe. Beyond that, the Holy Spirit is the person who is acting—sanctifying—in his explanation to the third article. Luther did set forth expectations for human behavior set by the creator in explaining the first article: all that God provides in this world "is done out of pure, fatherly, and divine goodness and mercy, without any merit or worthiness of mine at all. For this I owe it to God to thank and praise, serve and obey him." The life sanctified by the Holy Spirit, according to the explanation of the second article, is a life that Christ has taken possession of "so that I may belong to him, live under him in his rule, and serve him in eternal righteousness, innocence, and blessedness" on the basis of his resurrection.[3]

Luther's treatise *On Christian Freedom*, which he composed as the climax of his four programmatic treatises in 1520, has been labeled his greatest work treating justification—perhaps aside from his larger Galatians commentary. But this estimate ignores the fact that, in it, Luther discussed the Christian life under the power and guidance of the Holy Spirit a great deal. In fact, in this treatise he did not discuss or distinguish justification and sanctification as topics. He did write of the relationship of faith and works within the framework of his fundamental anthropological distinction of two aspects of human righteousness. His treatise reflected the mindset found in the first of his *Ninety-five Theses*: the entire Christian life is a life of repentance. For he had already come to the conclusion that Christians remain in combat with the sin that resides in them, even though God has pronounced them righteous on the basis of Christ's death and resurrection.

On Christian Freedom presumes that the trust the gospel elicits and sustains in believers will recognize that if God says they are righteous, then they will trust that they are truly one righteous person—to be sure in God's regard, but also in their own practice of their identity as his righteous children. Christ's liberation, the topic of this treatise, serves to break the bondage of human thinking, willing, and feeling

---

[3] BSELK 870–873, BC 354–356.

to every kind of idol, as it does to death the captivity under which idolaters live, and as it restores the righteousness and innocence of Eden to God's chosen people.

The freedom from idols that captivate us and define us as sinners comes through the work of Christ. It results, in Luther's words, in being bound to those with whom he's placed us in community. Perhaps "bonded" to them is a better choice of words. Luther felt compelled to demonstrate to his critics that his understanding of justification by faith alone did not mean that Christians were free to do anything they wanted, so he turned to the language of bondage. He might otherwise have chosen the language of "freedom for" being the creatures God fashioned his humans to be in the first place.

"Freedom" is a word of relationship. It demands a preposition. In German, "a relationship word" can take both "from" and "for" to describe the two relationships in which it functions. Christ's liberation *from* our captivating idols is repeated daily as we drown the old Adam. His liberation *for* true human living takes place as we "come forth and rise up to live before God in righteousness and purity that never ends."[4] These two aspects or events constitute what the Wittenberg theologians meant by "sanctification."

Our life of sanctification stems first of all from being freed from the captors who lead us into idolatry of all kinds, as we seek to find or to bolster and preserve our core identity by depending on alternatives to our creator in someone or something he has made. This continuing experience of Christ's liberation from those captors is called repentance: turning or being turned from the captivating dependence on the objects of the creator's artful hand back to the creator himself, as he has come to set us free through the death and resurrection of Jesus. The Old Adam has been judged and eliminated from God's sight when he looks at us. But in the mystery of the continuation of sin and evil in the lives of the baptized people of God, the Old Adam reasserts himself again and again, waving what Paul calls in Romans 7 "the law of sin" over our heads and weaving it into our hearts. It must be torn out and its accusation and condemnation thrown away every day because it is like the cat with more than seven lives.

---

[4] BSELK 884–885, BC 360.

A favorite motif in horror films is the coming back to life of a corpse. Formerly dead people usually seem to wreak havoc; they never spread happiness and joy. Christians experience this phenomenon each day as their sinful identity with all its tendencies surfaces again, although in baptism we have died to sin and our sinful identities have been laid into Christ's tomb and sealed there. Rather than master this mystery of the continuation of sin and evil in the lives of God's chosen people with our rational calculation, we can only master it with repentance—with another day of drowning the sinner in us. We can only master the reality of sin in our lives by enjoying the fact that the Holy Spirit causes our new person to come forth and rise up to live before God in righteousness and purity. That is a life of sanctified delight: delight in living under God's gracious favor and enjoying the life of love and service he designed for us in conversation with him and community with other human beings. In this world, where missing the mark continues to bedevil us, the dying that is presupposition for the fuller enjoyment of the blessings of God's gift of life never goes away. Dying to our sinful identity is liberation from eternal death. Thus, our daily "mortifying the flesh" is the way to true freedom.

"Mortification" is one of those words that have gone lost in our language—in fact, willfully abandoned by North Americans hell-bent on denying death. The insights of sociologist Ernest Becker in his description of a society determined to hide death from the consciousness of young and old (*The Denial of Death*, 1973) apply not only to physical demise but also to our spiritual death. The end of our existence as sinners is an accomplished fact; God's re-creative promise of life in Christ has set us free from the shadow of death. It anchors our new identities in his baptismal act of laying our sins in his tomb and giving us new birth as children of God (Rom. 6:3–11, Col. 2:11–15). That killing and restoration of righteousness is why he came into human flesh (Rom. 3:25). He has freed us by giving us a new identity as his newly reborn children. God has secured this new identity of ours in his own mind. It is not always so fixed and unshakable in ours. We find it easy to deny both the death that threatens because of the law's condemnation and also the death that God has executed in the death to sin of our baptisms.

We are confronted day in and day out with the mystery of the continuation of sin and evil in the lives of the baptized. Martin Luther found stimulus and impetus for combatting sin and evil in the baptismal promise when he wrote in the *Small Catechism*, "the old creature in us with all sins and evil desires is to be drowned and die through daily contrition and repentance, and on the other hand that daily a new person is to come forth and rise up to live before God in righteousness and purity forever." Living before God sounds good, but doing it in righteousness and purity is not always to the taste of the part of us captive to the law of sin, especially when that involves drowning and mortifying the sins and evil desires that keep on besetting us.

We sometimes hear the words, "I wish I were dead," from our own lips. Often it is only a moment of embarrassment or perhaps pains and aches that unleash such a phrase. But for others or for us all at one time or another, there are days, weeks, and years that impel some to actually mean that. But even then, some of those sinful idols are giving us more than pleasure. They become sources of our identity, wellsprings of our sense of security or safety, cradles of feelings that give our lives a notion of worth and meaningfulness for who we are and what we do. For those who mean it when they say, "I wish I were dead," God comes to say, "Do I have a deal for you!" In baptism, he presents us with an act of re-creation that frees us from our old identity as sinner and effects a total alteration in our core identity (Rom. 6:3–5, Col. 2:12). Then, in company with the Holy Spirit, we face the challenge of making that identity express itself in our daily interaction with our creator and with the creatures he has placed within our reach.

God has given all his people his Word as they find themselves in the frontlines of his combat against Satan and all his minions. That combat is fought out on the battlefields of the individual lives of believers. Each believer finds in the proclamation of both gospel and law powerful support in the task of combatting the tempter and our idols each day. This drive toward victory takes place even as remnants of that false impression of who we are raises the ugly heads of temptations of all kinds. Both pleasure and trepidation, anxiety and desire lure us away from the obedience of faith. Against these lures and traps that attempt to impose our former identities as sinner upon us, Christ liberates us from the oppression of our sin through both the promise of the gospel and the directives of the law. As Melanchthon reported in his coverage of this war of liberation, the law—God's design for human life—always accuses, even when we are not listening.[5] As Luther notes in the *Smalcald Articles*, the law always crushes,[6] even when we do not identify where the pressure is coming from. Even when God's exposition of what faith in Christ produces in our lives is being consulted by a sanctified will in search of more than the information that the sanctified mind can construct, the law shifts quickly to focus on what we have not done in accord with God's design. But such execution of sinners through the execution of God's judgment upon straying children who have landed in Satan's jail prepares the way for true Christian freedom, the freedom to live in truly human fashion.

Believers hear God's pronouncing them righteous, and their passive reception of this gift of righteousness—despite appearances of many kinds—convinces them that God knows who he is talking about. If God has given me a declaration of righteousness, I must regard myself as righteous, and so I go about enjoying that righteousness by actively pursuing his will. But the temptations continue to gnaw, lure, undermine, entice, and ensnare. Repeating the promise of new life in Christ, reiterating the gift of the presence of the Holy Spirit in our lives, retelling the story of Christ's death and resurrection—all these have the liberating effect of baptismally enlivening us and putting to death the fresh manifestations of the desires of our sinful selves. The repetition of God's design for our lives plays its role in mortifying the flesh and unshackling the child of God as well.

We find ourselves captive to both sins of commission and sins of omission. The Holy Spirit unfetters us from their subtle powers by reasserting our identity as those freed for holy living. He unties these cords by pointing out the possibility for discovering new paths of exercising our freedom with directives and examples, both general and specific. From one another we seek models for identifying what in our lives is distracting us from trusting completely in Christ and what is luring us into abuses of our own humanity. For we need

---

[5] BSELK 282–283, BC 126.
[6] BSELK 750–751, BC 312.

help and practice at identifying the source of the power of specific sins over us. We need to identify why some of those abuses are so attractive and why some things intimidate us to the point that we do not venture into specific ways of serving others and sharing the joys of the gospel. With sharper perceptions of what is fouling our nests and why we enjoy contaminating ourselves with certain practices or feel compelled to abstain from bringing the joys of service to ourselves and others, we can better dampen the fires that lure us into self-indulgence and that scare us off from aiding others. Christ has released us from captivity to the desires to stoke those fires.

Finally, mortification looks forward to the vivification that the Holy Spirit is yearning to enact in our lives. There dare not be left room for seven devils to enter into the spot where some sin has been cast out. God's Word of liberation moves from the admonitions that kill to the life-giving identification of us who hear it as children of God. That takes place as he constructs the framework for new habits and dispositions that exhibit the gift of the righteousness. This is the gift that defines the freedom to live in truly human, godly fashion. We aid each other in cultivating the replacements that fill the time and supplant the motivating forces that Satan has been claiming as his own and directing according to his destructive plans for us.

In his *Large Catechism*, Luther describes the emancipation of his people that Christ accomplished in his death and resurrection. He answered the question, what does it mean that Jesus has become my Lord? by writing:

> It means that he has delivered [literally "unfettered"] and released me from sin, from the devil, from death, and from all misfortune. Before this I had no lord or king, but was captive under the power of the devil. I was condemned to death and entangled in sin and blindness.
>
> For when we were created by God the Father and had received from him all kinds of good things, the devil came and led us into disobedience, sin, death, and all misfortune. As a result, we lay under God's wrath and displeasure, sentenced to eternal damnation, as we had merited it and deserved it. There was no resource at our disposal, no help, no comfort for us until this only and eternal Son of God, in his unfathomable goodness, had mercy on us because of our misery and distress and came from heaven to help us.

But he did come to help, as Luther continues his story.

> Those tyrants and jailers have now been routed, and their place has
> been taken by Jesus Christ, the Lord of life, righteousness, and every
> good and blessing. He has snatched us, poor lost creatures, from the
> jaws of hell, won us, made us free, and restored us to the Father's favor
> and grace. As his own possession he has taken us under his protection
> and shelter, in order that he may rule us by his righteousness, wisdom,
> power, life, and blessedness.
>
> Let this be the summary of this article, that the little word "LORD"
> simply means the same as deliverer [often translated "redeemer" but
> the word "erlösen" in German has the sense of loosing the bonds
> holding a prisoner], that is, he who has brought us back from the
> devil to God, from death to life, from sin to righteousness, and keeps
> us there [this is the justifying turn from sin to righteousness, with the
> resultant sanctified life as righteous child of God]. The remaining
> parts of this article simply serve to clarify and express how and by
> what means this redemption was accomplished—that is, how much it
> cost Christ and what he paid and risked in order to win us and bring
> us under his dominion. That is to say, he became a human creature,
> conceived and born without sin, of the Holy Spirit and the Virgin, so
> that he might become Lord over sin; moreover, he suffered, died, and
> was buried so that he might make satisfaction for me and pay what I
> owed, not with silver and gold but with his own precious blood. And
> he did all this so that he might become my LORD. For he did none of
> these things for himself, nor had he any need of them. Afterward he
> rose again from the dead, swallowed up and devoured death [two of
> Luther's favorite expressions], and finally ascended into heaven and
> assumed dominion at the right hand of the Father. The devil and all
> his powers must be subject to him and lie beneath his feet until finally,
> at the Last Day, he will completely divide and separate us from the
> wicked world, the devil, death, sin, etc.[7]

Christ has obtained victory in order to free us from our captors of all
kinds; Luther's favorite list of "devil, world, and flesh"—a trio prominent in Christian thinking for at least 1,200 years at his time—could
be placed alongside the law's condemnation and God's wrath as that

---

[7] BSELK 1054–1059, BC 434–435.

which bound us and kept us from God. In addition to images of liberation from sin, rebirth or new creation as children of God, death under the law's condemnation and subsequent resurrection, Luther used biblical language of reconciliation, for instance. One Latin word for "priest" is *pontifex*, literally bridge-builder. Our high priest has built the bridge that frees us from the perils of the other side, and he leads us across that bridge, which he has laid down over turbulent waters, back to the Father. Escapees from self-imposed alienation from his benevolent rule, we land as refugees whom he integrates into his way of governing life.

What is this way of life for which we are set free? What shape does "freedom for genuine human living" take? Luther's *On Christian Freedom*, like his treatment of *Two Kinds of Righteousness* and *On Good Works* in the months before its publication in late 1520, had not separated liberation from our evil captors from our freedom for true human living. Luther insists that only through trusting God's word of absolution do we "attain"—or, better, "receive"—righteousness in God's sight. Luther added that the trust that fulfills the fundamental element in God's design for human life: the fearing, loving, and trusting God above all things set forth in the first commandment. Trust thus fulfills the works of all the other commandments.[8] This trust, Luther asserts, "is born and preserved by preaching why Christ came, what he brought and gave, and what are the needs and the fruit that his reception entail. This kind of preaching occurs where Christian freedom, which we gain from him and which makes us Christians all kings and priests, is rightly taught."[9] For the proclamation of Christ's liberation opens up true life by convincing us that God has rendered us righteous through the death and resurrection of Christ and through his own regard or reckoning of that work of Christ to our accounts. As Luther often noted, our own new life is like the origin of all that exists. God spoke, and reality comes into being. So also in the words of absolution.

What does this kind of trust really mean? Luther explains in *On Christian Freedom*:

---

[8] *The Annotated Luther*, ed. Timothy J. Wengert (Minneapolis: Fortress, 2015, [henceforth AL]), 1:502.

[9] AL 1:508.

> The inner person—conformed to God and created in the image of God through faith—is joyful and glad on account of Christ, in whom all good things have been conferred upon such a person. Because of this, that person has only one concern: to serve God joyfully, with boundless love and with no thought of earning anything. While acting this way, immediately the inner creature offends a contrary will in its own flesh, one that serves the world and tries seeking after what belongs to it. Because the spirit of faith cannot tolerate this at all, it attempts with joyful zeal to suppress and coerce the flesh.[10]

Here Luther acknowledges the struggle that takes place over the disposition—the emotional state—of believers. He focuses, however, on the joy that comes to everyone who has been held captive under oppressors of any sort.

Joy is not a word that has automatically been associated with sanctification in all Lutheran circles. It is where Luther's focus falls. Unlike many of his followers in subsequent centuries, Luther was an exuberant man, with a personality filled with deep emotions. He possessed a personal disposition that led him to see more clearly than most, apart from the psalmists, both the darkness and horror of evil of all kinds and the exaltation and the exultation that come with being acquainted with a God who loved us to death. Trust in God and joy at experiencing the result of his speaking to us and acting in our behalf by dying and rising inform and form the freely lived, sanctified life.

Luther wrote the script that lays the foundation for the believer's way of thinking:

> A Christian should think as follows: "Although I am unworthy and condemned, in Christ, my God devotes to my insignificant person, without any merit and by sheer gracious mercy, all the riches of righteousness and salvation, so that I need absolutely nothing else further except faith, which believes that it is so. Thus, to such a Father as this, who overwhelms me with these his inestimable riches, why should I not freely, joyfully, with a whole heart and willing eagerness do everything that I know is pleasing and acceptable to him? Therefore, I will give myself as a kind of Christ to my neighbor, just as Christ offered

[10] AL 1:511.

himself to me. I will do nothing in this life except what I see will be necessary, advantageous, and salutary for my neighbor because through faith I am overflowing with all good things in Christ."[11]

This overflowing life is not a life of "doing it my way" or "standing on my own two feet." It's a life woven according to God's plan and Christ's pattern into the warp and woof of human community around me. In the *Small Catechism*, where Luther sketches a plan for daily prayer, he advises believers to "go to your work joyfully." He was simply repeating the emphasis on the enjoyment of serving that others receive from following the example of Christ and spending life in bearing the crosses of others and sharing our joy with them.

The English word "satisfaction" comes from the Latin "making enough," and "fulfillment" indicates being filled to the top. The German translation of "satisfaction" is *Zufriedenheit*, which means "at peace-ness." Freedom to be human because Christ has liberated us from trying to create our own version of being human means that he gives us freedom for enjoyment of his determination of what is enough for us, what truly fills us, what sets us at an Edenic peace. That peace we enjoy is the satisfaction of service to others, in the fulfillment of emptying our lives of those things that block us from imitating the providing and protecting God who nourishes us and gives us peace and joy by filling us with such emptying.

Joy-filled freedom is exercised within the horizons for human life set by its creator. Believers do the works God has designed for the good human life. In Luther's words, this is "in compliance to God out of spontaneous love, considering nothing else than the divine favor to which the person wishes to comply most dutifully in all things."[12] He focuses more on the good works that bring joy in the horizontal dimension of daily life, but Christians also recognize the joy and peace that come from praying, praising, and giving thanks to God and from gladly hearing and learning God's Word.

In *On Christian Freedom*, Luther spends no little time in urging believers to care for and discipline their own bodies in order to have

---

[11] AL 1:523–524.
[12] AL 1:512.

the capacity to carry out God's commands. He directs the reader's attention, however, to the foundational axiom that

> a human being does not live in this mortal body solely for himself or herself and work only on it but lives together with all other human beings on earth. Indeed, more to the point, each person lives only for others and not for self. The purpose of putting the body in subjection is so that it can serve others more genuinely and more freely. . . . It can never happen that in this life a person is idle and without works toward one's neighbors. . . . In all of one's works a person should . . . be shaped by and contemplate this thought alone: to serve and benefit others in everything that may be done, having nothing else in view except the need and advantage of the neighbor.[13]

This is a life of hearkening to the voice of the creator and re-creator—trusting that we have truly been freed from the bonds of sin and for the bonding of righteousness—placing us into the family of our God. In this family, God has claimed the role of protecting and providing parent, in whose image we have been made and remade, and whose way of life we joyfully reflect.

Luther sketched the nature and framework of this life with his understanding of the structure of callings in the societal structures of his time—although he altered that understanding in several significant ways. In the *Small Catechism*, Luther provided for those going to confession the way to use this framework to prepare for confession of sins: "Reflect on your walk of life [calling] in the light of the Ten Commandments." He then sketched the structure of Christian callings that shaped his "Table of Christian Callings" at the end of his Catechism: father, mother, son, daughter, master mistress, servant. Then he went on to summarize the commandments: "whether you have been disobedient, unfaithful, lazy, whether you have harmed anyone by word or deed, whether you have stolen, neglected, wasted, or injured anything."[14] On the positive side of the commands, Luther found the proper way to practice one's callings in life. These are the fields of freedom and

---

[13] AL 1:519–520.
[14] BSELK 884–885, BC 360.

the activities that express the freedom to be fully human for which Christ has set us free.

The medieval understanding of society placed each individual in one or the other of the three "walks of life" or "estates"—situations—of life. Luther came to argue that all people are placed in all three. Implicitly, in the *Small Catechism*, he contends for four estates, since he recognized both family and economic responsibilities in the walk of life labeled "household" (*oeconomia*). Furthermore, Luther uses the term *vocatio* to refer to the proper designation for responsibilities that God has assigned to all, even if only Christians recognize them as callings from their creator.

The economic aspects of being a faithful member of the *oeconomia* provide an example of how Luther tried to cultivate this life of freedom for being truly human—for finding joy in serving others as a form of praise to the creator. The explanation of the first commandment notes that among our most formidable captors, who imprison us in very cruel ways, is "Mammon."

> There are some who think that they have God and everything they need when they have money and property; they trust in them and boast in them so stubbornly and securely that they care for no one else. They, too, have a god—mammon by name, that is, money and property—on which they set their whole heart. This is the most common idol on earth. Those who have money and property feel secure, happy, and fearless, as if they were sitting in the midst of paradise. On the other hand, those who have nothing doubt and despair as if they knew of no god at all. We will find very few who are cheerful, who do not fret and complain, if they do not have mammon. This desire for wealth clings and sticks to our nature all the way to the grave.

Luther counsels clinging to God with one's whole heart as the only means to receiving the one eternal good.[15] Then we become channels through which God blesses and provides for others and fills our lives and theirs with thanks.[16]

---

[15] BSELK 932–939, BC 387–388.
[16] BSELK 938–939, BC 389.

In dealing with our callings in the economic sphere of life in the seventh commandment, Luther concentrates on sinful abuse of God's material gifts. Christ has come to free us from indulging in such sinful abuse of material blessings by setting our confidence on the God whose love has been proven by the cross and empty tomb. The conclusion of his explanation to "you are not to steal," reminds readers of the joys to be had in exercising economic responsibilities as the image of the providing and caring God.

> Anyone who seeks and desires good works will find here more than enough things to do that are heartily acceptable and pleasing to God. Moreover, God lavishes upon them a wonderful blessing, and generously rewards us for what we do to benefit and befriend our neighbor, as King Solomon also teaches in Proverbs 19 [:17]: 'Whoever is kind to the poor lends to the LORD, and will be repaid in full.' Here you have a rich Lord, who is surely sufficient for your needs and will let you lack or want for nothing. Thus with a happy conscience you can enjoy a hundred times more than you could scrape together by perfidy and injustice.[17]

Being turned into or onto ourselves for our economic security and for establishing the significance of our lives on the basis of what we possess or what gives us the gusto of fleeting pleasures is nothing more than bondage to that which will rust and rot.

But according to Luther's explanation of the seventh commandment, that is what servants and employees do when they "waste things or are negligent with them in order to vex and annoy" their employers, or do so simply out of carelessness. Artisans—plumbers, electricians, roofers, for example—both overcharge and, despite that, are "careless and unreliable in their work," Luther complains. "At the market and in everyday business the same fraud prevails in full power and force. One person openly cheats another with defective merchandise, false weights and measures, and counterfeit coins, and takes advantage of the other by deception and crooked practices and crafty dealings." They "swindle . . . fleece, skin, and torment" customers. He then goes on to criticize those with greater economic power,

---

[17] BSELK 1016–1019, BC 419–420.

like the bankers who drove his parents to the edge of bankruptcy or into it as they were striving to establish their smelting operation in Mansfeld. In addition, courtiers—bureaucrats—gouge the poor with their taxing system. Luther is calling for economic justice at every level of society—tax relief for the poor and not for the rich—and is demanding its exhibition in every Christian life.

By establishing himself as our Lord, Christ has freed us from every need to depend on our own efforts and anything else in his creation. This freedom from such dependencies has liberated us for the practice of the righteousness that his death and resurrection have pronounced upon us. Christ has emancipated us from the compulsion to secure our own eternal life with good works and the compulsion to secure our daily life by amassing his material blessings for ourselves. My economic security lies in the one who has, according to the *Small Catechism*'s explanation of the first article of the Creed, "given me and still preserves my body and soul: eyes, ears and all limbs and senses; reason and all mental faculties." In addition, he "daily and abundantly provides shoes and clothing, food and drink, house and farm, spouse and children, fields, livestock and all property—along with all the necessities and nourishment for this body and life." And even more, he "protects me against all danger and shields and preserves me from all evil." For he has "done [this] out of pure, fatherly and divine goodness and mercy, without any merit or worthiness of mine at all!"[18]

Luther observes this basis for our security often in his sermons. The freedom for using material gifts for the neighbor's need is demonstrated, for instance, in Jesus's feeding of the four thousand in Mark 8:1–9. This, Luther tells his hearers and readers, reveals that God "is a rich and powerful lord and provider; indeed, he is a rich miller and baker, better than any other upon the earth that has learned his trade perfectly. . . . He plows, harvests, threshes, grinds, and bakes in a twinkling of the eye."[19] By supplying the tax payment to Peter in Matthew 17:27, Jesus further illustrates how God continues

---

[18] BSELK 870–871, BC 354–355.

[19] *D. Martin Luthers Werke* (Weimar: Böhlau, 1883–1993, [henceforth WA]), 22:120,18–28; *Luther's Works* (Saint Louis and Philadelphia: Concordia and Fortress, 1958–1986, [henceforth LW]), 78:257; *The Complete Sermons of*

to create and give in the midst of daily life, for he brings bread and water out of rocks.

> We are to be sure familiar with the fact that grain grows yearly out of the earth, and through this familiarity we are so blinded that we do not esteem such work. For what we see daily and hear, that we do not regard as miraculous. But indeed it is just as great. To speak correctly, it is a greater miracle that God should give us grain out of the sand and the stone than that he here feeds the masses with seven loaves.[20]

On this basis, we as employees can recognize our responsibility to produce faithfully and fully for the benefit of our employer's business, even when the employer treats us poorly. Luther cast employers into a parental role, commanding that they have parental hearts toward those who work for them. He did not countenance exploitation or abuse of household servants or those employed in artisans' shops or merchants' warehouses.[21] For our service in this calling as worker serves not only the employer but also customers, fellow workers, and perhaps investors, as well as the wider public who profit from the business. As the sanctified children of God, rejoice that we are able to use the opportunity to earn wage or salary through honest and dedicated conduct of our tasks with the gifts and skills God has given us.

Our economic callings demand honest and faithful treatment of customers when we serve them for repairs and installation of household items, and that responsibility extends to responsive and cordial dealing with those whom we serve. For we view them as people to whom God has sent us to love through our skilled, care-filled service. Those of us who are merchants are concerned for proper products that serve the best interest of our customers. We who are professionals strive to demonstrate God's providing concern through our own careful attention to the application of law or the application of medical means at our disposal or the application of engineering

---

Martin Luther, ed. John Nicholas Lenker (1905–1909; Grand Rapids: Baker, 2000, [henceforth CP]), 4:218; 78:257.

[20] WA 22:120, c35–121,22, CP 4:219, LW 78:257–258.

[21] BSELK 980–981, BC 406.

principles to the tasks that God has assigned us through the social structures of our time.

Luther does not help us much with dealing with the situations in which we walk through life as part of institutions and systems in which we have very limited control. He criticized bankers for abusing their callings from God, but he did not address how bankers already in his day were being caught up in the larger system of developing capitalism. He criticized courtiers for their maltreatment and exploitation of their ruler's subjects in peasant villages and in expanding towns, but he did not see the larger web in which they were trapped as early modern forms of government lurched toward the absolutist state of the seventeenth century. Christians today must deal with the captivities brought upon us by these institutions and systems in which we become trapped by forces beyond our control and decision-making. Furthermore, our material blessings provide us in Western Europe, North America, and Australia more formidable traps and cages for more of us than for Luther's contemporaries. Disposable income is always an invitation for turning in upon ourselves in self-indulgence. The crying needs of the poor in every land challenge us to responsible exercise of our callings as consumers, and our accountability for the gifts God has given us call upon us to careful thinking about that which we spend and the producers whose products we purchase. Christ's assurance that God has freed us from every captor that turns us in upon ourselves permits us to live the life of freedom that finds joy in serving others, not only with direct, face-to-face service, but also with cash contributions that meet human needs thousands of kilometers away.

Such examples could be multiplied for every walk of life: in our families we are freed from the need to protect ourselves so that we can truly sacrifice for spouses, children, parents, and other relatives immediate and more distant. As citizens of our municipalities or counties and of our nations, we can joyfully pay taxes for the common good and can cast votes that seek the welfare of the city, as God commands in Jeremiah 29:7. As members of congregations, we recognize that we are called to support and love those who worship and serve with us as God's closer family and give time and dedicate skills and time to the common joy in the gospel which we enjoy together.

Christ has set us free from every captor that turns us in upon ourselves so that we are freed for the life truly sanctified by the Holy Spirit. That life grasps the full enjoyment of our humanity, the fulfilling and peace-bestowing satisfaction that results in our living with total confidence in his liberating gift of life, after existence under sin's dominance and Satan's lordship had been squeezing the life out of us. Since Christ has set us free, every aspect of our lives—even in the struggle with the law of sin each day—can be free indeed. Thanks be to God, we freely say, through Jesus Christ our Lord, who through his victory over our captors has liberated us for today and for eternity. That is the ultimate significance of our sanctification.

Baptism and the Freedom
of a Christian

John T. Pless

There are no explicit references to baptism in Luther's *The Freedom of a Christian*.[1] Yet Luther's teaching on the nature of faith and the life of the Christian as a life lived outside of the self in Christ and the neighbor certainly has striking parallels with Luther's teaching on Holy Baptism. We might first keep in mind that in the same time-frame that Luther writes on *The Freedom of a Christian*,[2] he was also thinking and writing about baptism. In the year prior, he penned *The Holy and Blessed Sacrament of Baptism* and, in 1520, *The Babylonian Captivity of the Church*. In the 1519 treatise, Luther is still working within the Augustinian framework where baptism consists of three

---

[1] Here see the discussion in Brett Muhlhan, *Being Shaped by Freedom: An Examination of Luther's Development of Christian Liberty, 1520-1525* (Eugene: Pickwick, 2012). Muhlhan observes Luther's "dynamic, threefold view of baptismal faith and the relational impact baptism had before God, the self and the neighbor" (40) undergirding his theological understanding in *The Freedom of a Christian*. Here also see Robert Kolb, *Luther's Treatise on Christian Freedom and Its Legacy* (London: Lexington/Fortress, 2020), where he argues that Luther was not explicit in his treatment of baptism in this treatise because he assumed that most of his readers were familiar with his arguments in *The Babylonian Captivity of the Church*, written earlier in 1520 (35).
[2] A brief but helpful historical overview is given by Mark Tranvik, "The Freedom of a Christian (1520)," in *How the Reformation Began*, ed. Anna Marie Johnson and Nicholas Hopman (Eugene: Pickwick, 2022), 72-80.

parts: *signum* (the thing signified), *res* (the thing itself), and *fides* (faith). In *The Babylonian Captivity of the Church*, Luther now speaks of baptism not as legal symbol or a sacrament of works but of justifying faith.[3] Luther comes to see that baptism does not just symbolize the believer's death and resurrection but that baptism is an actual death to sin and rising to the newness of life in Christ.

Luther's teaching on Holy Baptism comes to fruition in the catechisms, and it is from them, particularly the *Large Catechism*, that we see the connections with *The Freedom of a Christian*. Here we see Luther making baptism "present tense." It is no longer in the rear view mirror as a rite of initiation that gets you on the salvation track! Baptism encompasses the whole of the Christian's life. There is a very potent statement in the *Large Catechism* (*LC*):

> In baptism, therefore, every Christian has enough to study and practice all his or her life. Christians always have enough to do to believe firmly what baptism promises and brings —victory over death and the devil, forgiveness of sin, God's grace, the entire Christ, and His Holy Spirit with all his gifts. In short, the blessings of baptism are so boundless that if our timid nature considers them, it may well doubt whether they could all be true. Suppose there were a physician who had so much skill that people would not die, or even though they died would afterward live eternally. Just think how the world would snow and rain money upon such a person! Because of the throng of rich people crowding around no one else would be able to get near. Now, here in baptism there is brought free of charge, to every person's door just such a treasure and medicine that swallows up death and keeps people alive.[4]

Key in this section are the words "what baptism promises and brings." Luther focuses on four points: (1) victory over death and the devil; (2) forgiveness of sins; (3) God's grace and the entire Christ; (4) the Holy Spirit with all his gifts. The liberating efficacy of baptism is nothing other than the work of Christ himself.

In his explanation of the Creed's second article, Luther confesses that Jesus "has redeemed me a lost and condemned person from all

---

[3] See Luther, *The Babylonian Captivity of the Church*, in LW 36:65.

[4] *LC* IV 41–43, *BC*, 461–62.

sins, from death, and the power of the devil. He has done this not with gold or silver, but with His holy, and precious blood, and with His innocent suffering and death that I may be His own and live under Him in His kingdom and serve Him in everlasting righteousness, innocence, and blessedness." Now the language that Luther uses in the second article comes to expression in the *Small Catechism*'s explanation of the benefits of baptism: "it works forgiveness of sins, rescues from death and the devil, and gives eternal salvation to all who believe this."

Even as the atonement is Christ's work and not our own, so too is baptism! Luther never tires of stressing this in the *Large Catechism*: "To be saved, as everyone well knows, is nothing else than to be delivered from sin, death, and the devil, to enter into Christ's kingdom, and to live with him forever."[5] This is freedom. Christ has liberated us. We are no longer in captivity to sin, death, and the devil. They are not my lords; Jesus is.

Just as in the *Small Catechism*, there is a parallel to the second article. Consider the dramatic language when he explains what it means that Jesus has become my Lord: "It means that he has redeemed and released me from sin, from the devil, from death and all misfortune. But before this I had no lord or king, but was captive under the power of the devil. I was condemned to death and entangled in sin and blindness."[6] Again, just a few lines down: "Those tyrants and jailers have been routed, and their place has been taken by Jesus Christ, the Lord of life, righteousness and every good and blessing. He has snatched us poor, lost creatures from the jaws of hell, won us, and made us free, and restored us to the Father's favor and grace. As his own possession he has taken us under his protection and shelter, in order that he may rule us by his righteousness, wisdom, power, life, and blessedness."[7]

This freedom of the Christian is baptismal freedom. Christ Jesus gives the gift of freedom in baptism and received in faith. Faith does not make baptism, but it is by faith alone that we receive the benefits of baptism. At this point, we might also note the connection with

---

[5] *LC* III 25, *BC*, 459.
[6] *LC* II 27, *BC*, 434.
[7] *LC* II 30, *BC* 434.

The Freedom of a Christian where Luther employs the imagery of marriage. He writes

> Now let faith intervene and it will turn out that sins, death, and hell are Christ's, but grace, life, and salvation are the soul's. For if he is the groom, then he should simultaneously both accept the things belonging to the bride and impart to the bride those things that are his. For the one who gives his body and his very self to her, how does he not give his all? And the one who receives the body of his bride, how does he not take all that is hers?[8]

Luther calls this a "delightful drama." It is indeed a blessed exchange or a sweet swap, to use the colorful phrase of Robert Bertram.

The liberation Christ Jesus accomplished on the cross is given to you in baptism. What a gift this is, for it unites you with Christ! Luther says that, with the "wedding ring of faith," Christ now regards our sins as his very own "as if he himself had sinned, suffering, dying, and descending into hell—then as he conquers them all and as sin, death and hell cannot devour him, they are devoured by him in an astonishing duel. For his righteousness is superior to all sins, his life more powerful than death, and his salvation more invincible than hell."[9] The promise is sure and certain. Baptism makes it concrete, for here God has located his name by the word in the water, and whoever calls upon that name will be saved. In *The Freedom of a Christian*, Luther says: "But now it is impossible for her sins [that of the bride] to destroy her because they have been laid upon Christ and devoured by him."[10] If you step outside your baptism, you are back with your own sins where there is no freedom, but only bondage. The ship of baptism is unsinkable, but if you jump overboard, you drown.[11] The life of Christian freedom is lived *in* baptism, not apart from it.

---

[8] Martin Luther, *The Freedom of a Christian*, in *The Annotated Luther*, vol. 1: *The Roots of the Reformation*, ed. Timothy J. Wengert (Minneapolis: Fortress, 2015, [henceforth *FOC, AL*]), 500.

[9] *FOC, AL* I:501.

[10] *FOC, AL* I:501.

[11] Here see Oswald Bayer, *Martin Luther's Theology: A Contemporary Interpretation,* trans. Thomas H. Trapp (Grand Rapids: Eerdmans, 2008), 268–269.

In the *Large Catechism*, Luther speaks of the Christian life as a continual return to baptism. To the *Small Catechism*'s fourth question—"What does such baptizing with water indicate?"—Luther answers: "It indicates that the Old Adam in us should by daily contrition and repentance be drowned and die with all sins and evil desires, and that a new man should daily emerge and arise to live before God in righteousness and purity forever." Here Luther includes Romans 6:4 with the declaration of our death and resurrection with Christ in the *Large Catechism*: "Thus a Christian life is nothing else than a daily baptism, begun once and continuing ever after."[12]

Jonathan Trigg speaks of the circularity of the Christian life.[13] You don't outgrow your baptism. Rather, you continue to grow into your baptism by living in daily death to sin and daily rising to the newness of life in Christ. In *The Freedom of a Christian*, Luther argues that it does not help the soul if the body is adorned with priestly vestments, enters into sacred places, or performs holy works.[14] Baptism is a clothing of a completely different type. Hence the *Large Catechism*: "Therefore let all Christians regard their baptism as the daily garment that they are to wear all the time."[15] Clothed in the new, stripping off the old, baptism is the Christian's freedom because it is the pledge and promise that if the Son sets you free, you will be free indeed.

---

[12] *LC* IV 66, *BC*, 465.

[13] See the discussion in Jonathan Trigg, *Baptism in the Theology of Martin Luther* (Leiden: Brill Academic Publishers, 2001), 170–171. Also see Bayer's comment: "Baptism marks the intersection of the old world and the new. Ethical progress is only possible by returning to Baptism." Bayer, *Living by Faith: Justification and Sanctification*, trans. Geoffrey Bromiley (Grand Rapids: Eerdmans 2003), 66.

[14] See *FOC, AL* I:490.

[15] *LC* III 84, *BC*, 466.

Bound and Free:
Christ as the End of the Law
in the Life of the Christian

James Arne Nestingen

Luther took the phrase, "Christ, the end of the law," from Romans 10:4. Writing in New Testament Greek, the apostle Paul describes Christ in these terms: "He is *telos nomou*." He is the end of the law. The word "end" is capable of different interpretations. There's a sense of termination: "He is the stopping of the law." There's also a sense of fulfillment: "He is the one in whom the law is finally fulfilled." And so, as Luther hears it, the two words go together: Christ has fulfilled the law, he has terminated it, and he has stopped it. And so what we want to do is work through this and see how Luther is using these words. This became a slogan of the Reformation. Luther loved the sense in which the law *stops*, but he was also convinced that Christ fulfills the law. And precisely because Christ is the fulfillment of the law, he has also terminated it. But Luther uses the words in a very special sense, and that's what we're going to explore here.

Paul's claim that Christ is the termination of the law is part of a whole argument in his writings in which he reduces the law to a provisional reality. Christ Jesus has reduced the law to a provisional standing so that it holds limited authority. The argument is very simple. If Christ saves, he alone saves—and the law can't do that. If Christ is the way, the truth, and the life, then the law isn't and can't be. If the law was given for a good purpose, it was given for a provisional purpose. And so we see in Galatians how Paul likes to insult the law. The law was given through a mediator. Christ came out flat forward, outright to us. And so the law was, and is, the rude disciplinarian, the rude servant who goes with the kids to school and keeps them in line, pulls their ears, and spanks them with the ruler. You've seen this. Some of us, unfortunately, remember it. Getting the discipline of the teacher for messing around too much, right?

So the law is not the teacher. The law is not the professor. The law is not the principal. The law is a disciplinarian that's been retained to keep order in the classroom so that the teacher can teach. And so Paul, throughout Galatians and his epistles generally, can't find enough ways to insult the law. He wants to remind us that it's only for sin. It was not given for righteousness. It was given for discipline, but not to teach. It was given to keep order in the classroom so that the teaching could happen. Christ as the end of the law is part of this whole argument Paul makes in which the law was not given for righteousness, nor does it define righteousness. Christ defines righteousness, and so the law is deaf, dumb, and mute.

Paul wants to retain the sense of the law's termination. Christ brings the law to a full stop. Jesus says, "That's it. That's far enough, law. You've done enough now." And when he says that, he does something else again that's very important. So we're going to have to look at two things here. We're going to have to look at the end to see how Paul can get away with saying stuff like this, and how Luther can follow him, and secondly, once we've done that, then we're going to have to look at the new arrangement. We are no longer under the law, but under the power of the gospel, and so under the power of the Holy Spirit.

The author of the Gospel of John does not use the phrase "end of the law," like Paul does, but he tells a story in John 20 in which the law does end, putting us under a different power. That is the power of the Holy Spirit. And this, I think, is one of the greatest stories in all of scripture. You know that the disciples did not do too well according to the Passion narrative. Before Jesus prepared to go to Jerusalem to suffer and die, they were full of all kinds of stuff, seeking to advance themselves. They got into arguments about who was the greatest of the apostles and who was really going to provide the leadership. They got into all kinds of monkey business about which one of them was the closest to Jesus and which one of them had had the biggest advantage. And so we hear about the disciple Jesus loved, and we hear about other disciples contending for this status.

As we see the story of the Passion starting to move towards an end, things get more and more serious, and the disciples have more and more trouble. They're under the squeeze now. They're seeing what's going to happen. The Gospel of Mark says it flat out: They all forsook him and fled. All of them took off—and one of them in such a hurry that he ran right out of his toga and streaked the whole community. He ran away naked because he didn't want to get caught. He didn't want to be found with Jesus. And so the story of the resurrection begins with the disciples hiding for fear of the Jews. Of course, this is in keeping with their bad behavior. This is not any great achievement on their part. They know what we all know, that if you get the head man, then you get the other leaders as well. So Jesus has been arrested, and they're anticipating arrest by the authorities. That will be the end of it. So this is the apparent end of the story, right?

Jesus has been arrested, tortured, and killed. All of the disciples are cowering, hiding in the upper room in Jerusalem. They're scared to death. They don't know where to go or what to do. And they're accusing themselves, no doubt. They have failed. You can imagine Peter has some hard memories. As Luther used to say, it wasn't a big Roman soldier that scared Peter into denying Jesus. It was an acne-scarred fourteen-year-old. She didn't say, "You're a follower of Jesus." She said, "Aren't you from Galilee? Doesn't your accent give you away?" She figures he's betrayed himself just by his speech. When Peter hears that, what does he do? Well, he jumps up and down and denies: "I don't know him. I never saw him."

That's the memory that he has in mind as he sits in that room wondering if the authorities are going to catch up with them. He's being accused relentlessly, but not because Jesus or the authorities have shown up. It's because he remembers his failure. The apostles have all forsaken Jesus and fled. They didn't stand with him valiantly, confessing their faith. They went down one by one, shamefully and shamelessly. And now they're hiding and have time to think and reflect. They're accused by their own consciences. Now, this is the work of the law. Law is whatever accuses, as Luther says. In this age, among sinners, the trademark of the law is its capacity for accusation.

When you have the sense of having betrayed someone—your spouse, one of your kids, a sister or brother or a friend—when you have that sense and feel accused by it, that's the law in the conscience. That's what the law does; it always accuses. That's its characteristic power and its characteristic trick.

Now, this is the beginning of the church. A bunch of guilty disciples hiding in a room, scared to death that the Romans are going to find them. This is apostolic succession. This is what happens if you count on human powers; it all goes in the hole. Now, there's a big discussion of why Jesus just walked in on them—why he didn't stand at the door and knock. You know that great saying, "Behold, I stand at the door and knock." Well, he didn't do that here because he knew what would have happened if he'd knocked. There'd be ten disciples piled one on top of the other in front of the door to make sure he couldn't get in.

So he doesn't knock. He goes right through the wall. When he enters the room, he says the most surprising thing of all: "Peace be with you." Not only that. He says it again. He says it twice. Undoubtedly, he knew, as we do, that the first time they heard it, the disciples wouldn't be able to believe it. He knows that they're guilt-ridden and fearful. Even for him whose word creates worlds, guilt is such a power that it's going to stop any communication. And so Jesus says, "Peace be with you," and he says it again. This is the end of the law. This is the termination of the law. When the law loses its power to accuse, it's not the law anymore. When the law loses its capacity to shame and humiliate and destroy, it's not the law. Peace be with you is a form of absolution. To pronounce peace is to say that your sin is forgiven for Jesus' sake.

This is Christ now speaking; he's blessing you. When he blesses you in this way, the law ends. It's lost its power. It can't accuse you anymore. Its mouth is stuffed. It has to shut up because it's lost the capacity to accuse. Christ has taken over, even though you are a sinner who has been found guilty. When Christ says, "Your sin is forgiven," or, "Peace be with you," he is blessing you with the hope of the gospel. He is releasing you from everything that could be held against you. In your heart of hearts, you might say, "But I betrayed him." In your heart of hearts, you might say, "But I have these memories of sins from my youth." And yet Christ says, "Peace be with you." The law has lost its power to accuse. When the law can't accuse anymore, it's dead. It's lost. Now, Luther doesn't use the word *dead*, but says that the law has gone *in vacuole*. The law has gone into a vacuum and has lost its power to accuse.

The argument is almost complete, but there's a second important move. The law has ended, but now Christ Jesus goes another step. He breathes on the disciples and says, "Receive the Holy Spirit. If you forgive the sins of any, they are forgiven. If you retain the sins of any, they are retained." Here we see the power of the risen Christ. He not only stops the law, but he fulfills the law. He fulfills it by breathing into the disciples the power of the Spirit. This is very much like the Genesis story. When God created Adam, he breathed. He gathered the dust, and he breathed into Adam and Eve the breath of life. So now Christ breathes into his shattered, despondent, and guilt-driven disciples. He forgives their sins and breathes into them the power of the Spirit.

Just a minute ago, they were hiding under the horrific attack of the conscience. They betrayed the one and only; they let him down. But now, Christ has forgiven them. "Peace be with you," and when he says this, he breathes on the disciples and says, "Receive the Holy Spirit. If you forgive the sins of any, they are forgiven. If you retain the sins of any, they are retained." This is the power of the gospel. The Holy Spirit works through the word of the gospel and takes hold of the heart. He creates faith when and where he pleases in those who hear the gospel.

When Jesus breathes on the disciples, he doesn't give them a handbook. He doesn't give them a list of rules and regulations. He gives the Holy Spirit. And now Peter the betrayer becomes the rock he was originally meant to be. Peter the betrayer is in the grip of Jesus Christ, now a witness of the gospel. And the same is true with Paul. "And last of all, to me as to one untimely born, chief of sinners though I be." That's what the Holy Spirit does. He convicts us of sin and righteousness. So when the Holy Spirit gets ahold of you, he turns you inside out. You can't maintain any false pretenses anymore. You know you're a sinner.

But when the Holy Spirit gets ahold of you, he convicts you of righteousness and blesses you so that you know from the inside what Christ is after—true freedom of the gospel. In Christ, we are free from all accusations: from sin, death, and the power of the law. The Christian is completely free from the law. It has come to an end. But being free from the law, you are free under the power of the Holy Spirit to be of some earthly good, to be of service to your neighbor. So the end of the law is one of the great slogans of the Lutheran reform, even though it makes people mad. We are free from the law indeed; but the law has ended so that we can be of service to others. Without handbooks or rules and regulations, we now can bear witness to Christ Jesus and hand over his benefits to any and all. What greater joy could there be?

The Preached Word: Certainty and Freedom

John J. Bombaro

Luther taught pastors, and all Christians, to have a mutual esteem for the authority of God's word, written and preached. But it was the latter (preached and proclaimed) that he asserted is divine and efficacious speech. He even built this view into the *Small Catechism*, explaining the third commandment with these words: "Remember the Sabbath day by keeping it holy. *What does this mean?* We should fear and love God so that we do not despise preaching and his word, but hold it sacred and gladly hear and learn it."[1] Luther sees preaching as synonymous with God's word: it is God's authoritative and powerful speech. And so it can be as certain as the written word in its presentation of freedom from divine judgment, along with the freedom one has in a life indwelt by the Holy Spirit.

God's Word: Written and Spoken

There is a certain tension between Luther's view of Scripture per se (the Bible itself) and the gospel as God's "external word"—by which the reformer meant the proclamation of the gospel in all its liturgical forms. This also includes the administration of the sacraments as other external words of God. The sacramental word is the fully

---

[1] Luther, *Luther's Small Catechism with Explanation* (St. Louis: Concordia, 2017), 13.

authoritative word of God based on the written word. They are not in conflict but work in complementary fashion, with the latter necessarily and exclusively dependent on the former. Finnish theologian Uuraas Saarnivaara explains that

> Luther did not see any conflict between his conviction that Scripture is the normative word of God, and that God bestows His grace and forgiveness of sins by means of the spoken word and sacraments. All preaching and administration of the sacraments have their source in the written word of God and must take place according to it. Therefore, the proclamation of the word (in sermons and in personal absolution and counseling) and the administration of the sacraments is inseparably connected with the Scriptures. Only a scriptural teaching, preaching, and consolation lead men to the knowledge of Christ and salvation in him.[2]

In the *Smalcald Articles* (1537) Luther writes: "We ought and must constantly maintain that God does not wish to deal with us otherwise than through the spoken word and the sacraments, and that whatever without the word and sacraments is extolled as spirit is the devil himself" (*SA* 3, 8). This is a basic belief found throughout Luther's writing and is held by those true to the Reformation tradition: God forgives sin through the proclamation of the gospel.

In this teaching, Luther was unwavering: "The oral word must— before anything else—be present and be grasped with the ears if the Holy Spirit is to come into the heart, who enlightens us through the word and works faith."[3] Likewise, he writes:

> There is no other way to have sins forgiven than through the Word. . . . The Lord, our God, has not promised to forgive our sins than through any other work that we do, but He has connected it with the unique work of Christ who has suffered and risen from the dead. This work He has, through the word, placed it in the mouth of the apostles and the ministers of the Church, and in cases of emergency of all Christians,

---

[2] Saarnivaara, "Written and Spoken Word: Luther's View," *Lutheran Quarterly* 2, no. 2 (1950): 169.

[3] WA 29:581, cited in Saarnivaara, "Written and Spoken Word, 163.

to the end that they through it would distribute and proclaim the forgiveness of sins to those who desire it.[4]

The Reformation rightly understood this teaching to arise directly from Scripture itself. Paul clearly taught that "Faith comes by hearing and hearing through the word of Christ" (Rom. 10:17), where the "word of Christ" is the gospel. Faith comes from hearing the gospel. This, of course, is in keeping with Paul's admonition to Timothy to "Preach the word" of Christ.

Proclamation, Not Just Information

Of greater significance, the authoritative word proclaimed is in keeping with the dominical example of preaching the gospel as the means of salvation and sanctification (Mark 1:39; 2:2; Luke 4:44; 20:1). Jesus doesn't just preach the Bible. He commissions preachers to proclaim in his stead and with his authority. He doesn't commission the disciples to conduct Bible studies per se. But since he establishes a relationship like that between a king and his ambassadors, the commissioning pertains to heralding the royal decree: hence "[his disciples] departed and went through the villages, preaching the gospel" (Luke 9:6). This royal mandate to herald the king's "good news proclamation" through the external word is the apostolic commission. The only word commissioned was the word of Christ and him crucified. They had no authority to preach any word but the king's word.

What we find in Acts is resolute confidence that God dispenses faith and fortifies faith in the preaching of the gospel according to Jesus. Acts essentially narrates Paul's teaching that "Christ Jesus . . . became to us wisdom from God, righteousness and sanctification and redemption" (1 Cor. 1:30). And so all of the apostles engaged the world through preaching the gospel of Christ Jesus—the king's message about the king himself:

- "And every day, in the temple and from house to house, they did not cease teaching and preaching that the Christ is Jesus" (Acts 5:42).

---

[4] WA 52:273, cited in Saarnivaara, "Written and Spoken Word," 167.

- "And the twelve summoned the full number of the disciples and said, 'It is not right that we should give up preaching the word of God to serve tables'" (Acts 6:2).
- "Now those who were scattered went about preaching the word" (Acts 8:4).
- "Now when they had testified and spoken the word of the Lord, they returned to Jerusalem, preaching the gospel to many villages of the Samaritans" (Acts 8:25).
- "But Paul and Barnabas remained in Antioch, teaching and preaching the word of the Lord, with many others also" (Acts 15:35).
- "Some of the Epicurean and Stoic philosophers also conversed with him. And some said, 'What does this babbler wish to say?' Others said, 'He seems to be a preacher of foreign divinities'—because he was preaching Jesus and the resurrection" (Acts 17:18).

Note that the preached word was not merely *information*, but *proclamation*. Information is just secondary speech about Jesus. But proclamation is primary speech. It is Christ's word because it comes from him. But he's also the one speaking the word by proxy, through his royal agents—those called, commissioned, and ordained to do so.

Therefore, this word is powerful, not because it's moving, compelling, or profound. Rather, the power is in the fact that it is the sword of the Spirit. It's a performative, active word from the Lord that accomplishes the purposes God intends. The power is God's, and God applies his word when the gospel is preached. The promise of that power, Luther says, is bound to and limited by the word of the gospel of Christ. Thus Paul admonishes the Corinthians: "I decided to know nothing among you except Jesus Christ and him crucified" (1 Cor. 2:2). Here, then, we have a rationale for what Paul writes in Romans 10:12–17:

> For there is no distinction between Jew and Greek; for the same Lord is Lord of all, bestowing his riches on all who call on him. For "everyone who calls on the name of the Lord will be saved." How then will they call on him in whom they have not believed? And how are they to believe in him of whom they have never heard? And how are they to hear without someone preaching? And how are they to preach unless they are sent? As it is written, "How beautiful are the feet of those who preach the good news!" But they have not all obeyed the

gospel. For Isaiah says, "Lord, who has believed what he has heard from us?" So faith comes from hearing, and hearing through the word of Christ.

Here we must observe the strong emphasis on preaching the "good news." This gospel is "the word of Christ"—the king's royal proclamation of himself.

With such clear teaching from Scripture, Luther puts the emphasis on the spoken word for justification and sanctification. But when it comes to the norm and rule of our faith and life, his emphasis is on the written word of the Bible. He often says that the gospel in its essence is the spoken, proclaimed word. "The Gospel must be a living voice" because the one, true, holy, catholic, and apostolic church is a "mouth-house" not a "pen-house." Luther would go so far as to equate preachers with "the mouth of the Holy Spirit" when they externalize the gospel.[5] This is what preaching certainty is all about—a clear understanding that the word proclaimed comes from the highest authority and is itself an authoritative word regarding the status of the baptized as to their freedom from divine judgment and everlasting death.

Lutherans confess this doctrine of the Bible in the *Smalcald Articles*: "In those things which concern the spoken, outward word, we must firmly hold that God grants His Spirit of grace to no one, except through or with the preceding outward word. Thereby we are protected against the enthusiasts, that is, spirits who boast that they have the Spirit without and before the word . . . as they boast that they have received the Spirit without the preaching of the Scriptures" (3, 8). The Reformation's insistence on this teaching arises directly from great confidence in God the Holy Spirit to work through the dynamic word that is Christ and him crucified as it encounters believers and unbelievers alike, changing states of affairs and making new realities. This is the heralding and sacramenting of the king's word that accomplishes the purpose he intends.

The royal decree—Christ and him crucified for our sins—must be externalized from the page of Scripture. The *Augsburg Confession*

---

[5] WA 40II:410, 2 Hs. (=Handschrift or manuscript text), cited in Saarnivaara, "Written and Spoken Word," 172.

puts it this way: "By the word and sacraments, as by instruments, the Holy Spirit is given, who works faith; where and when it pleases God, in them that hear the Gospel. . . They condemn the Anabaptists and others who think that the Holy Ghost comes to men without the external Word, through their own preparations and works" (Article 5). This teaching preserves the reliability, objectivity, and undeniability of the written word *and* the Holy Spirit for justification and sanctification. Certainty comes not through examining one's works, but through the word proclaimed as the word of the Lord himself.

It is faith—not knowledge—that is the instrument through which salvation comes and sanctification occurs. Both certainty and the freedom that follows arise from the word engendering and stirring faith. Knowledge doesn't hold the same place as faith when it comes to justification and sanctification. Faith believes God and his promises—including the promise that, in the hand of the Holy Spirit, God's word creates and sanctifies. Therefore, the Reformation tradition invests divine authority in the preached word of Christ. This word is authoritative and active. That's why preaching—the sermon—bridges the two high points of a true Lutheran liturgy: the reading of the gospel and the celebration of Holy Communion.

This brings us back to the difference between *primary* and *secondary* speech in preaching. Lutherans don't emphasize preaching because of its explanatory and informative nature. Rather, Lutherans emphasize preaching because it's primary speech. Preaching is a direct address, one person to another: you are forgiven, you are baptized, you, take and drink. In this way, the central elements of the divine service—the reading of the gospel and celebration of Holy Communion—are bridged by the sermon, which addresses sinners with the message from Christ himself. This is applied to each person because Christ intends to address all those sitting before him in the congregation.

Mission and Proclamation

In *The Gospel in a Pluralist Society*, Lesslie Newbigin argues that understanding "the missionary mandate" as primary obedience to a command misses the point of the Gospels and Acts, and operates by a law kind of logic, rather than a gospel-logic. The same thing, of course, applies to preaching, since the missionary mandate consists mainly in the proclamation of the gospel, leading to Holy Baptism. The major lesson here is that missional preaching is the work of the Lord when it is the Lord's word that's proclaimed. And if it is the Lord's word that's being proclaimed, then the sermon doesn't belong to the preacher. Missional preaching lives in the domain of grace, not human persuasion. When this is the case, preaching becomes a joyous endeavor for the preacher and his listeners. Such joy colors the proclamation itself and stimulates certitude in its message.

The crucified Christ is now seated at the right hand of God until all things are put under his feet. Preaching is about making that fact a certitude for those who hear. This must be proclaimed because it is the truth about reality. It's a fact of history. Preaching Christ in this way brings calm and repose in those who listen because of the certainty that Jesus is in charge. This is the heart of the Christian conviction: our king and savior was crucified and died, but having now been raised, he rules and reigns by the power of the Holy Spirit through grace, mercy, truth, peace, and love. The truth about God's kingdom breaking into our fallen world is that this is *good news*. It's a message delivered with joy. We rejoice that God reigns though Christ according a new covenant of grace, not the old covenant of law. That's nothing other than the bread of life for beggars like us.

The key to understanding missions and preaching is that it's Christ's mission and message. Christ commissions the message of the kingdom of God. You're not at liberty and there's no freedom of religion when it comes to preaching. Consequently, it isn't the preacher's sermon that's preached, but the message that comes from Christ. This should be clear from the fact that preachers can't save anyone. Salvation is the Lord's work. It's not merely a past-tense accomplishment during the first-century coming of Jesus. It's also a present accomplishment delivered to us through the gospel. The Lord's work is accomplishing salvation, but the same is also true of its present application.

For our part, "going" and "preaching" sets the stage in which the Spirit brings the saving faith of Christ to needy sinners and strengthens the faith of sinners saved by grace. Jesus states that this is the way it is going to be when *his* word is preached—when *his* sermon is your sermon:

> The Lord appointed seventy-two others and sent them on ahead of him, two by two, into every town and place where he himself was about to go. And he said to them, "The harvest is plentiful, but the laborers are few. Therefore pray earnestly to the Lord of the harvest to send out laborers into his harvest. Go your way . . . and say to them, 'The kingdom of God has come near to you.' . . . The one who hears you hears me, and the one who rejects you rejects me, and the one who rejects me rejects him who sent me (Luke 10:1–3, 9, 16).

When the sermon is Christ's proclamation of the kingdom of God, then the result is "Whoever receives you receives me, and whoever receives me receives him who sent me" (Matt. 10:40). Receiving Christ is pure joy—it's the joy of being certain of one's freedom. Therefore, the mission of preaching arises from the dynamics of the gospel.

This means that the mission of preaching isn't only a matter of teaching. It's also a matter of learning that the word of the Lord is the work of the Lord. He provides both the mandate and the motivation for missional preaching. This comes from the Holy Spirit, for the fruit of the Spirit is joy (Gal. 5:22). Preachers can therefore be confident in the word of Christ, and so, being dependent on him, they can have joy in God's mission. Joy in God begets mission, and mission perpetuates the joy that comes from the gospel.

Good Pastoring and Good Preaching

Paul did not preach into a vacuum. Because he was so personally invested in the lives of his auditors, Paul's listeners received his words as a message from someone with the right to speak into their lives. At the same time, because Paul was an apostle of Christ, his writing and preaching were imbued with the authority of the king, and received as such. But Paul's apostleship comes with an enhancement: his personal love and care for his auditors and readers was embraced as Christ's own love and care. The apostle and the pastor, therefore, embody Jesus' own affections for the people committed to their pastoral care.

Authentic pastoral care optimizes the potential reception of the word of Christ preached.

Thomas Oden applies this to contemporary preaching when he says, "The quality of communication that will enable the renewal of the church and ministry today must be both apostolic and personal, both a rich recollection of the tradition and a highly personalized communication of that tradition through specific relationships of caring."[6] When love, concern, emotive closeness, and personal engagement characterize the preaching to the bride of Christ, it is inherently authoritative and familiar—the address of the bridegroom to his bride. He loves her in a deeply sacrificial way, always with her betterment, salvation, and sanctification in view (cf. Eph. 5:25–32).

Luther beautifully brings together authority and personal relationship when he paraphrases Paul's opening salutation in 1 Timothy:

> My dear Timothy, you know me. . . . You know my teaching. You have observed all of the many things I have suffered and the false brothers I have had. You have seen from how many directions spies have set up attacks on me. And you know, too, that I have no hope other than Christ. You have worked together with me in persecution, and you know that I trust no man. So I write to you in a more familiar fashion, because Christ is our Hope.[7]

Luther speaks from a tradition that has, at least historically within Lutheranism, distinguished itself by authentically Christ-like pastoral care, established by and through an unwavering commitment to true biblical doctrine—preserved in the documents of the *Book of Concord*. Such things lend themselves to the stimulation of faith and, by extension, personal assurance and confidence of the freedom we have in Christ as the justified.

Preaching is enhanced by teaching from a posture of pastoral love and passion for the salvation and sanctification of those in the

---

[6] Thomas C. Oden, *First and Second Timothy and Titus, Interpretation: A Bible Commentary for Teaching and Preaching* (Louisville: John Knox Press, 1989), 18.

[7] LW 28:218.

pastor's care. A pastor's reputation among his people shapes their reception of the word. This is why outstanding pastoral care is not merely a companion to good preaching. Likewise, sound preaching is not just a complement to faithful pastoral care. Both are necessary. Authentic proclamation must have both truth and love. When both are present, the word's authority grows in the hearts and minds of Christians. His sheep know his voice and follow him (John 10:2–6; 10:27). Implied in John's words is the fact that the sheep know the Good Shepherd's love and care in his voice, for the two are blended into one. Authentic proclamation is therefore the love of Christ for souls communicated through the care of his undershepherds.

Certainty and Freedom Come from the Word

Both law and gospel are serious—and preaching them seriously adds the certitude and freedom to live as the Lord's own. The law is serious because "through the law comes knowledge of sin" (Rom. 3:20) and therefore our guilt (Rom. 3:19), with its deadly consequences (Rom. 6:23). The gospel is serious because it declares that "when the fullness of time had come, God sent forth his Son, born of woman, born under the law to redeem those who were under the law" (Gal. 4:4–5), through "a propitiation by his blood" (Rom. 3:25). Stated together, preaching law and gospel—the full counsel of God—is serious business. Since "we have now been justified by his blood, much more shall we be saved by him from the wrath of God. For if while we were enemies we were reconciled to God by the death of his Son, much more, now that we are reconciled, shall we be saved by his life (Rom. 5:9–10).

Again, it is this seriousness that results in the joy of a solemn truth received: "More than that, we also rejoice in God through our Lord Jesus Christ, through whom we have now received reconciliation" (Rom. 5:11). Certainty, and the freedom it results in, is the important thing for Paul.

And so the message is serious, while the response moves from guilt and dread with the law to rejoicing and delight through the gospel. Yet the gospel itself is also a serious proclamation, though it is thoroughly infused with the joy of freedom.

In a courtroom, both the proceedings and the juridical pronouncement at the end are solemn affairs. The mood is one of reverence and awe, and rightly so: there is going to be a verdict, and it may not be welcome news. Likewise, preaching the word of the Lord will always include some damning accusation, some violation of the law, but it will also conclude with *good* news, a favorable declaration. The pastor, then, is to the divine service as the judge is to the courtroom: he embodies dignity and solemnity proportionate to the proceedings and pronouncements that take place there.

Preaching Freedom without Clichés

Preaching and catechesis go hand in hand to maximize Christian understanding, devotion, and appreciation of our holy faith. Indeed, there is preaching on the catechism (usually during the season of Lent), and there is preaching that is also catechetical. Both include "the basic principles of the oracles of God" (Heb. 5:12), but they also require more. To be sure, the Holy Spirit uses the law and gospel proclaimed, but the law-gospel distinction isn't the only interpretive principle emerging from Scripture. There are other useful principles, such as the metanarrative of Scripture. This requires explanation so that hearers are oriented to the context of law and gospel. This means preaching the overarching story of Scripture, with all its internal complexity, and not one's own story.

Preaching that employs the clichés of modern politics and entertainment culture, does not and cannot convey the "solid food" of theology, doctrine, typology, and cruciform thinking, because it is milk. And such milk does not develop the believer toward maturity, "for everyone who lives on milk is unskilled in the word of righteousness, since he is a child" (Heb. 5:13). Like Paul and the preacher of Hebrews, every theologian of the cross should strive to bring the people of God to maturity in teaching *and* preaching, for "solid food is for the mature, for those who have their powers of discernment trained by constant practice to distinguish good from evil" (Heb. 5:14). This should be the goal of every preacher: to placard the story of God in Christ for the world with ever-increasing insight from the whole of Scripture and enacted through the liturgy so as to bring the baptized into greater degrees of maturity.

Minimalistic, shallow, and trite preaching in lockstep with consumerist expectations forgets that Peter didn't offer a snappy "God is my copilot" or "have your best life now" homily to his Pentecost hearers. Rather, "with many other words he bore witness and continued to exhort them" (Acts 2:40), so much so that his sermon ended with sacramental action: "So those who received his word were baptized" (Acts 2:41). Such things don't happen with words better suited for a T-shirt than a pulpit. Peter's "many other words" added a depth-dimension to the word of God, manifesting its multifaceted and paradigmatic subject: God in Christ reconciling the world to himself. Deference is due to the preacher not because he is the subject matter expert (although he should be). Nor is deference due because the pastor is the equal of those who listen, with an expectation of reciprocity in another context. Rather, in preaching, the pastor fills an office on behalf of an authority. And it is to this authority that all must give deference, for this authority is none other than the rightful king of heaven and earth. Therefore, a posture of decorum and receptivity must characterize a proper Lutheran mass.

Preaching Justification and Regeneration Together

Christian freedom isn't merely juridical. It's also real, because it comes off the pages of Scripture to us through the sacramental application of the word. The result of this is regeneration.

Preaching the sinner's justification by God's grace alone through faith alone on account of the work of Christ alone is the core of the gospel. This was the light of the Reformation that shone into the darkness of works-based medieval Catholicism. But that gospel core is like a chemical compound—there's more than one element to it. Salvation is constituted by *both* justification and regeneration. These two elements must be distinguished, to be sure. Regeneration is the result of justification. But distinguishing these two parts of salvation doesn't mean they should be divorced from one another.

The ontological regeneration of the sinner must be preached alongside forensic justification. God's justifying word recreates the sinner in Christ, not just by reckoning the sinner one with him, but by actually uniting the sinner with the one who is the source and substance of eternal life (John 11:25). Such life isn't just a quantity of time, like life-everlasting, but a quality of existence. Eternal life with Christ is the divine life into which the baptized are initiated. Justification and regeneration are necessarily connected and have profound implications for the craft of preaching.

Preaching justification by faith should not exclude the truth of regeneration, as if justification were a separate phenomenon that took place sometime before, with regeneration taking place sometime later. Equally erroneous is the idea that regeneration establishes the basis for justification, as if there were something about the sinner that merits justification. Christ is always and only the basis of our justification. He alone is our righteousness (Jer. 23:6; 33:16; 1 Cor. 1:30). There is no righteousness to be had apart from Christ our Lord—both in justification and sanctification. But being declared righteous for the sake of Christ carries the implication that we have now, by the power of God, been regenerated: our life is now "hid in Christ in God" (Col. 3:3). This double declaration infuses preaching with a vitality toward urging the pursuit of holy living by eschewing the antinomian idea that we can live as we please, as if God's law were entirely defunct.

The double declaration is important because many preachers skittishly avoid preaching regeneration, fearing they might sound legalistic, and thus slip into the error of gospel-reductionism. Christ expects Christian living from Christians; otherwise, he would not have made us new. Being reckoned righteous in Christ and having Christ in us (Gal. 2:20–22) means that our sanctification is affective and suffused. The Spirit of Christ acts in us doing works of righteousness (Eph. 2:10; 4:24; Titus 2:14), none of which we can boast of as our own (Gal. 6:14). Christ also graciously transforms our hearts (Rom. 8:29; 12:2).

Preachers shouldn't fear articulating the ethic of Christ's kingdom from the pulpit. The ethics of his kingdom are the expectations of our king, whose Spirit indwells the baptized to be "zealous for good works" (Titus 2:14). The preacher shouldn't fear articulating the consequent good works that Christians do for the church and their neighbors. These things follow the miraculous work God does *to* us (regeneration) when he declares something *about* us (justification). The consequence of justification includes a life of piety, the pursuit of holiness, a love for other Christians, devotion to the Trinity, truth-telling, the struggle against the flesh, and the good works required by our neighbors in our various vocations.

The people of God need to hear the truth, comfort, and joy of regeneration, so that they don't lapse into thinking there are no expectations of the justified person. Quite the opposite: regeneration says you are a new creation with a new king living in a new kingdom. Justified sinners have a new standard for authentic human living in the form of a kingdom ethic that is brought by the Spirit of that same Christ "who became to us wisdom from God, and righteousness and sanctification, and redemption" (1 Cor. 1:30). Let the whole people of God hear the whole counsel of God from the pulpit—the law that exposes our sin, the gospel of God's grace in Christ, and regenerate life in the church. The dual themes of justification and regeneration allow the preacher to proclaim the good news of the gospel and articulate the reality of living as resurrection people in the here and now.

Conclusion

Lutheran preaching purposes to re-establish the truth of Scripture that the word of God accomplishes what it says. The efficacious word establishes new states of reality, as the will of the all-authoritative one proclaims freedom predicated upon the certainty of Christ's accomplished and applied redemption. Preachers and auditors of the word should have therefore the greatest confidence that God's primary speech *for us* obtains, with secondary speech enriching our understanding with information about the proclamation that liberates and regenerates.

Freedom in Luther:
From What and To What?

Knut Alfsvåg

Freedom is a phenomenon that is difficult to define. We know perfectly well what it is to be unfree. We know about difficult relationships and tight deadlines. But sometimes all limits and borders disappear, and we can do what we want. The difficult relationships disappeared. Assignments were completed and there were no more deadlines. We can do what we like. What do we do then? Suddenly we have a day to our disposal, a day we had planned for some chore that disappeared. Or we may be at liberty regarding the decisive questions in life. What do we want to do with lives when there are no other demands to be met first? If you can use your days and your time as you want to, what do you do then? This is certainly a question about freedom.

The question is made more complicated by our social context. As modern Westerners, we live in a context that emphasizes personal freedom. The individual should be at liberty to do as he or she likes. This is a value that is highlighted in our culture. What we should do with this freedom is less emphasized. This is a situation many find stressful and confusing. We have a lot of freedom, and we know that this is something we should appreciate. For which purpose should we use this freedom? Celebrate the limits that have disappeared? Binge TV watching? Unending hours on Facebook or other social media? Chasing excitement or intoxication?

This experience of freedom without guiding principles is a deeply frustrating experience. Humans are created to belong in a context, and contexts always imply demands. The chase of freedom as lack of any limits is therefore a meaningless way of organizing one's life. Freedom cannot be void of content. The idea of absolute freedom is a meaningless idea.

This was understood already by the Greeks of antiquity. They therefore understood freedom as the possibility of actualizing one's inherent nature. Freedom is the possibility of manifesting one's given identity. Freedom is not limitlessness. Fish are free when they swim in the sea. For fish, the necessity of being in water is not a limitation, but a precondition for growth and development. A tree is free when it has water and nourishment. If it does not have its roots in deep soil, it withers. The attempt at liberating oneself from the context within which one belongs leads to death.

The important question for humans is therefore: How should we realize our inherent nature? In which medium should we live to grow and develop freely? The answer to that question is love. To develop freely and generously, humans must experience love; we must live in a field determined by loving relationships. This is the case for children, but it is also the case for adults. This is not a controversial answer. Even Jesus and biblical authors point to love when they speak about the essentials in life. However, they do it in a way that is characteristically different from the way many today speak about love. In the Bible, love is not primarily a feeling. Love is an obligation. You shall love your neighbor as yourself! Love is the context within which you must find yourself if your life shall be meaningful. Love and be loved! This is life's basic demand of you. Only then you are free to become who you are.

It was probably reflections along these lines that made Luther start his well-known book on the freedom of a Christian with the following statement, and then use half the book to unfold it: "A Christian is a perfectly dutiful servant of all and subject to all."[1] From the supposition that freedom is to do what you want to do, this is a strange statement. However, Luther is not a modern, Western person primarily concerned about individual freedom, considering liberty as the allowance to do what pleases him. He thinks in a biblical way, and he therefore has no problems in filling the second half of this book with biblical passages teaching us that the meaning of life is to serve one's

---

[1] Luther, *The Freedom of a Christian*, in LW 31:344.

neighbor. The goal, Luther says, is to be captured by love to the extent that one has "a joyful, willing, and free mind that serves one's neighbor willingly." A love like this "takes no account of gratitude or ingratitude, of praise or blame, of gain or loss. For a man does not serve that he may put men under obligations. He does not distinguish between friends and enemies or anticipate their thankfulness or unthankfulness, but he most freely and most willingly spends himself and all that he has, whether he wastes all on the thankless or whether he gains a reward."[2]

How does one become a free human being? It happens through the realization of one's inherent nature. And how does one realize one's inherent nature? By living in love and loving one's neighbor. A human being realizes its nature by swimming in love like a fish swims in the sea. This can be done in numerous ways. A fish lives in the sea irrespective of swimming northwards or southwards. The obligation to love one's neighbor can be realized in different ways. For this reason, the New Testament exhortations are not too specific and mainly focus on the general principles. "The fruit of the Spirit is love, joy, peace, patience, kindness, goodness, faithfulness, gentleness, self-control," Paul tells us in Galatians (5:22–23). It can be said even more briefly: do what you want as long as you do it lovingly.

However, this reticence toward being too concrete and specific is not the same as relativism. Fish can do whatever they want to do as long as they are in the sea, but they have nothing to do on dry land. Humans can realize the obligation of love in many ways, but it is still very easy to find examples of unloving behavior. One of the more complete lists of examples of unloving behavior is find just a few lines above the passage from Gal. 5 I just quoted. The actions that do not exemplify love, i.e., the actions that are the human variation of being a fish on dry land, are described by Paul in the following way: "sexual immorality, impurity, sensuality, idolatry, sorcery, enmity, strife, jealousy, fits of anger, rivalries, dissensions, divisions, envy, drunkenness, orgies, and things like these" (Gal. 5:19–21). This is an interesting combination of unloving attitudes, and different persons are affected in different ways by the phenomena Paul here addresses. Some of us have scarcely any problems with drunkenness and adultery but can have a lot of trouble when it comes to enmity, strife, and

---

[2] LW 31:367.

jealousy. Others may have no problems with the warning against envy but are affected by the warnings against sorcery and orgies. Love makes us creative, it is sometimes said. But even lack of love can be quite ingenious and works in different ways in different people.

This confronts us with a new problem. The human nature is to live in love. We realize ourselves by living according to the obligation of love. But we do not do that, at least not completely. We are not all affected by everything on Paul's list, but we are all affected by some of it. The complete realization of the obligation of love is beyond our possibilities. How can we then speak about freedom? Love should be a free realization of our inherent nature. But in reality this is a demand and an ideal of which we repeatedly fall short. What should be a life in freedom thus becomes a burden; it becomes a struggle for realizing an obligation we can never fulfil. How can we then realize a life in freedom?

Luther also reflected on this problem when he wrote *The Freedom of a Christian*. He therefore does not start by unfolding the obligation of love as I have done so far. He starts by declaring that love is the medium within which we already find ourselves: "A Christian is a perfectly free lord of all, subject to none."[3] The medium of love is a fact: it is the context, or the field, within we exist whether we like it or not. The context is given, and we are placed within it. Fish cannot first create the sea in which they swim—no more than we can create the area of love within which we live our lives. That is where we are before we have our first conscious thought. This has nothing do to with what we succeed or fail in doing; we live our lives within the confines of divine love whether we want it or not.

This is a fact, but we may have a hard time discovering it. Fish are hardly conscious of the significance of the sea within which they have always existed. In the same way, we are hardly conscious of the significance of the divine love within which "we live and move and have our being" (Acts 17:28). To have us understand the significance of the love within which we live, God must open our eyes to the reality of our life. This is something he does through the gospel, which in this way becomes the precondition for us being aware of the loving freedom within which we live. No contribution from our side can

---

[3] LW 31:344.

place us within the loving context in which we were created, but drastic measures may be necessary for us to understand that this is the place we are. When that happens, we can honor God as the origin of the field of divine love where our lives play out.

We need this recreation. We need to have our eyes opened. For reasons we do not fully understand, the good world God has created appears ambiguous. The implication of this is that we do not honor God as the origin of love and the giver of all good gifts. For this reason, we need to have our understanding of the world renewed so that we see the dimension of love within which we move when we realize our nature as it is meant to be. This understanding of divine love as the medium within we move in our lives is what Luther calls faith.

The life in conscious awareness of the reality of divine love is by Luther compared to a marriage. The soul is united with Christ "as a bride is united with her bridegroom."[4] Spouses have everything in common, and this is also the case with the soul's marriage with Christ. Through this marriage, the human then participates in Christ's grace, life, and salvation, and Christ receives the human's sin, death and condemnation. In this way we are still, incomplete as we are, able to freely move in the dimension of love as the medium of our lives. Through the soul's fellowship with Christ, we can accept the obligation of perfect love without collapsing under the burden. The obligation of love is valid under all circumstances. But even our half-hearted, unsuccessful attempts at fulfilling the obligation are carried by Christ's unconditional, infinite, and unchangeable love towards us. There is never anything to be added, because we exist within this dimension of unconditional love since the day we were created in our mothers' wombs. For that reason, we can even live with our futile attempts at realizing the commandment of love. Our position within the divine love is not affected by what we do or do not do. A marriage is not dissolved if the spouses do not always do what they should toward each other. This is also the case with the soul's marriage with Christ. It is a fairly robust construction, carried as it is by infinite, unchanging love.

I started by speaking about freedom but have ended up speaking mostly about love. The reason is that it is love, i.e., divine, infinite, and

---

[4] LW 31:351.

unchangeable love that is the answer to the two questions asked in the heading, the questions concerning what we, according to Luther, are free from and free to. What are we free from? We are liberated from our proclivity toward loveless egoism. What are we free to do? We are free to realize unconditional, undemanding love in our own lives. Primarily in our relations with the ones who are closest to us, spouse, children, and parents. Our closest relations are always the most important area for our realization of the commandment of loving our neighbors. Only two inter-human relationships are explicitly addressed in the Ten Commandments, and those are the relation between spouses and the relation between children and parents. But love of one's neighbor is not limited to the relation to the ones who are closest to us; it encompasses everybody with whom we come in contact throughout our lives.

This may always become a burden, and then freedom disappears. For that reason, a life lived within the dimension of loving one's fellow human beings should be nourished by the relation to God as the origin of love. We are placed within the area of divine love without any contributions of our own. Divine love is the innermost reality of the world, and this is something we can never change. But a life with God in prayer and worship is a precondition for experiencing it. This is the difference between humans and fish. Fish do not gather for worship, praising God for the water of the sea. They praise God by swimming in it. But with humans, who are created in the image of God, God wants a closer relationship. Therefore, he wants us to praise him for the loving relationship we are given to live in. Even though we praise God by living in this relationship, he also wants us to praise him by doing it consciously.

I will therefore end by doing just that, and for that purpose I have chosen one of the texts of the Bible that speaks clearly about God's unmovable love, here spoken of as his mercy, as the foundation of our lives, irrespective of how they are otherwise structured. Psalm 118:

> Oh give thanks to the LORD, for he is good;
> for his steadfast love endures forever!
> Let Israel say,
> "His steadfast love endures forever."

Let the house of Aaron say,
"His steadfast love endures forever."
Let those who fear the LORD say,
"His steadfast love endures forever."
Out of my distress I called on the LORD;
the LORD answered me and set me free.
The LORD is on my side; I will not fear.
What can man do to me?
The LORD is on my side as my helper;
I shall look in triumph on those who hate me.
It is better to take refuge in the LORD
than to trust in man.
It is better to take refuge in the LORD
than to trust in princes.
All nations surrounded me;
in the name of the LORD I cut them off!
They surrounded me, surrounded me on every side;
in the name of the LORD I cut them off!
They surrounded me like bees;
they went out like a fire among thorns;
in the name of the LORD I cut them off!
I was pushed hard, so that I was falling,
but the LORD helped me.
The LORD is my strength and my song;
he has become my salvation.
Glad songs of salvation
are in the tents of the righteous:
"The right hand of the LORD does valiantly,
the right hand of the LORD exalts,
the right hand of the LORD does valiantly!"
I shall not die, but I shall live,
and recount the deeds of the LORD.
The LORD has disciplined me severely,
but he has not given me over to death.
Open to me the gates of righteousness,
that I may enter through them
and give thanks to the LORD.
This is the gate of the LORD;
the righteous shall enter through it.
I thank you that you have answered me

and have become my salvation.
The stone that the builders rejected
has become the cornerstone.
This is the Lord's doing;
it is marvelous in our eyes.
This is the day that the Lord has made;
let us rejoice and be glad in it.
Save us, we pray, O Lord!
O Lord, we pray, give us success!
Blessed is he who comes in the name of the Lord!
We bless you from the house of the Lord.
The Lord is God,
and he has made his light to shine upon us.
Bind the festal sacrifice with cords,
up to the horns of the altar!
You are my God, and I will give thanks to you;
you are my God; I will extol you.
Oh give thanks to the Lord, for he is good;
for his steadfast love endures forever!

Free to Be a Living Being

Charles Lloyd Cortright

We are created as "living beings" (נֶפֶשׁ חַיָּה), in the words of Moses in Genesis 2:7. And in good Lutheran fashion, perhaps the best place to start is with the question, "What does this mean?" I'd like to answer this question by looking specifically at what Moses means—that's the "living being" part. Then I'll look at how Paul applies what it means for us to be *free* as living beings using his words in Romans 12:1. So, what does Genesis 2:7 mean when it says that we have been made "living beings"? Or better, what does it *not* say. In older English translations of Moses' words, this phrase was translated as "[Adam] became a "living soul." Some have pointed to this verse with the idea that this is what differentiated humanity from the rest of the animal creation because man is called *nephesh chayah*, the "living soul." And indeed, the Hebrew word *nephesh* can mean "soul." But the fact is, Moses' phrase in Genesis 2:7 is used to describe the biological life of human beings—something humans share with other "living souls."

Martin Luther noted this in his sermons on Genesis which he preached shortly after his return to Wittenberg from exile at the Wartburg in 1522. His sermons on Genesis given in 1523–24 fed into his later lectures on Genesis which he gave in the final decade of his life. Concerning *nephesh chayah* ("living soul"), Luther notes, "'And God the Lord made the man from the dust of the earth.' I have said above that God made a man and a woman; now I want to tell how it happened." To the question of what is meant by the term "living soul," Luther answers by distinguishing between the soul, as it was generally understood in western Christianity as spiritual life, and its meaning in the Old Testament.

In Old Testament usage, *nephesh* refers to "everything which lives in the five senses." Thus, Luther notes: "The Scriptures also call a fish that lives in water a 'soul' [Gen. 1:20] as it says in chapter one: 'Let the water bring forth living creatures (*animam viventem*).' Likewise, the birds of the air and the beasts which live on the earth are named the same way—as 'bodies which live' or 'living bodies.'"[1] So, the phrase *lebendige seele* (*nephesh chayah*) is the equivalent to that which is called "the natural life" (or in Luther's German, *das natuerliche leben*).

This is also Paul's meaning when he uses the term in 1 Corinthians 15:45. Quoting the Septuagint's Greek translation of Genesis 2:7, the apostle employs the terminology of a "living soul" (ψυχὴν ζῶσαν) to contrast Adam in his "natural life" with Christ, the "Last Adam" who is a "life-giving spirit" (πνεῦμα ζῳοποιοῦν). On the basis of Paul's comparison, Luther concludes:

> Paul's phrase "The first man was made a natural being" must be understood the same way [that is, as the "natural life"]. For he sets "living" and "spiritual" being against one another. The living being is this: a man hears and sees, smells, grasps, tastes, digests . . . propagates children, and does whatever else the body does as a natural being and function. That is what the Hebrew language calls "*seele*." So, we read in Exodus: "All the souls that were descended from Jacob were 70," that is, 70 children which were born to him. That is almost always the meaning throughout Scripture.[2]

Thus, Luther wants to distinguish between bodily life, such as was given Adam (and which is transmitted by propagation to humanity) and the spiritual life revealed in Christ (to which the faithful will ascend).

Genesis 2:7b, in other words, does not describe the spiritual life of Adam by calling him a "living soul," but only his natural, bodily life. So, Luther:

---

[1] WA 26:67.
[2] WA 26:67.

> Therefore, one cannot translate the word "soul" better than "the bodily life" or "a human being, who lives in a bodily life." Thus Adam is made in a natural life, but Christ, who is the "last Adam," says Paul, lives "in the spiritual life," that is, has a spiritual body so that he no longer eats or drinks, sees or hears like us, does no bodily thing or work, but is a quite different being and, indeed, a truer man, as we will be in that life.[3]

In biblical terms, then, we are talking about our lives in our bodies: free to be a living being, that is, free to live this life-in-our-body.

Now, what does this life for us Christians look like? Let me bring in the Apostle once again. In Romans 12:1, Paul says, "I appeal to you therefore, by the mercies of God, to present your bodies as a living sacrifice, holy and acceptable to God, which is your spiritual worship." To the question of what does it mean to live free, Paul reminds us that our freedom is not license to do whatever we want, but that we are free now to be what God meant us to be from the beginning. We are baptized. We are dead to sin but alive to God in Christ. And now what does it look like to be a sinner and a saint at once in daily life in the real world?

In a word, our freedom is a priesthood. The life of a Christian is a priesthood. And you are priests: priests in the royal priesthood of Jesus Christ, born and anointed in baptism to now freely offer your bodies as living, spiritual sacrifices. "I appeal to you therefore, by the mercies of God, to present your bodies as a living sacrifice, holy and acceptable to God, which is your spiritual worship." Notice how Paul's "therefore" here is a big deal. "Therefore" looks back at what he has said earlier in Romans: universal condemnation under the Law for Jews, Gentiles, pagans, you, me, everyone. He has also talked about the justification of humanity in the atoning death of Jesus.

"Free to be a living being" is founded in your baptism into that death. In Romans 6, Paul says our old self was drowned in baptism and that we have been buried with Christ. That old life is dead, but the true you is not! You are alive in Christ also in your bodily life. A *truly* living being. Notice also that we live a present paradox: being at once a sinner in Adam and a saint in Christ, with two wills at war

---

[3] WA 26:68.

within us. Flesh and spirit contend with each other even as the flesh goes to death and the spirit goes to life. All of this feeds into Paul's "therefore" and his appeal to live in the freedom of the new life which you now have. He also makes this appeal *by the mercies of God*. This is a not a law or a commandment, but an exhortation to be who you are in Christ. Christ offered his body as a bloody sacrifice. Now you are his baptized believer. But Paul also adds that you are also a baptized *priest*: so now offer your bodies as unbloody, living sacrifices of praise and thanksgiving.

This calls for a new way of thinking about freedom. The world's way of looking at it will not bring you to understand it. The world of science will not open your mind to it. The rhetoric of this age will not instruct you. These are the unseen and hidden things that must be revealed by the word. Paul defines our freedom this way: do not be conformed to this world and the way it thinks. You are in the world, but you are not of the world. Rather be transformed by the renewal of your mind—another way of speaking of our life of repentant faith. That is what the word "repentance" actually means. It means come to a new mind, a re-*cognition*, a transformation of that mind of yours which is in Christ Jesus, the mind which serves the law of God, as Paul says in Romans 7, even as the flesh serves the law of sin.

Now, no human priest is holy in himself. He must be washed before he takes up priestly service. He must be vested, covered in a robe that hides himself. In the Old Testament, a priest had to first sacrifice for his own sin before he could deal with the sins of the people. The blood that he sprinkled first had to fall on him. You were washed in baptism. You were clothed with Christ's perfect righteousness. He makes you holy. He anoints you. He washes you. He clothes you. He atones for your sin with his blood so that you can serve as his priest. It was one of the great insights of the Reformation—not new to Luther, but long forgotten—that every baptized, believing Christian is a priest before God.

But the word "priest" came to be synonymous with the office of the ministry and with the notion that only an ordained priest can offer a proper sacrifice. But ordination doesn't make a priest: ordination authorizes a pastor to speak on Christ's behalf. *Baptism* is what makes a priest. Priests are living beings in baptism. Ministers are made by call and ordination. The ministry is for this life and it remains only to the last day. But priesthood is eternal, and so you are priests forever in the order of Jesus Christ.

A priest never serves alone. You are priests in a royal priesthood just as you are members of one body. There is no such thing as an individual, isolated believer in the scriptures. No matter which image of the church you choose—citizens of a kingdom, stones in a temple, members of a body, priests in a priesthood—the biblical view of the believer is always that you are part of a larger whole. Even when you pray by yourself with the doors locked and it is just you and your Father in heaven, you say, as Jesus taught, "*Our* Father." "Give *us* this day *our* daily bread." Even alone, you always pray in the plural—with "us" and "we"—because, as a baptized priest, you are always in the spiritual company of your fellow priests in Christ the high priest.

There's a great danger at work in the church today, and it's the individualization of Christianity at the expense of the community of the church. Faith has become all about me and my personal life with Jesus. But that's the old Adam talking, not the new creature. The old Adam is the *me-first* narcissist who always approaches this life as *my* life lived for *me*. This kind of self-oriented, self-centered spirituality always puts *me* at the center. And this must be recognized for what it is: the heart-curved-inward is the very condition we call "original sin." And so much that goes on in the name of religion today actually panders to the sinner rather than the saint.

When you come together with your fellow priests to hear and receive and to pray, praise and give thanks, you are living the free life Paul is talking about in Romans 12: offering your bodies as a living sacrifice. Priests pray. They offer sacrifices. They give thanks. And when you do *not* gather, then one of the priests is missing. Everyone has to sing louder to make up for the loss. And absence discourages rather than encourages your fellow priests in their priesthood. Congregations are built one member at a time, and congregations die one member at a time. Every member that checks out sets the stage and example for the next one to do the same. And one by one, the church shuts down because the priests are not at their station. They're priests gone AWOL, and that doesn't make for much of a priesthood.

As living beings, you have gifts. God does not leave his priests empty-handed. Each of us is gifted in some way for the common good of the whole. The thing about gifts is that it's better to have others tell you about how you are gifted than to decide this for yourself. Have you ever run into someone who thinks they have a nice singing voice but really doesn't? Or who think they are really good at speaking when they really aren't? It's like hearing your own voice. Remember the first time you ever heard a recording of your voice? It can be a bit off-putting. It doesn't sound like you to you! You might ask people, "Do I really sound like that?" And they shake their heads and say, "Yes, that's exactly how you sound." And you're mortified. You always hear your voice through the bones in your head. You're the only one who hears your voice that way. Everyone else hears you like your recorded voice.

It's hard, if not impossible, to be objective about yourself. Paul says when you consider your gifts, think soberly and humbly, with the measure of faith God has given you. But know this. You are gifted by God as a member of Christ's priesthood. Your life in this body is to have a gift to offer to God by giving to your neighbor, to offer your body as a living sacrifice. U.S. President John F. Kennedy once famously said, "Ask not what your country can do for you; ask what you can do for your country." We could imagine that Paul might say it this way: ask not what the body of Christ can do for you, but ask what you—as a member of the body and a priest in the priesthood—can do for the body of Christ. The church is where you learn to receive and be nothing but given to. It's where you learn to give yourself away, because in Christ you are free and have nothing to lose.

These gifts Paul talks about may look rather mundane, ordinary, not terribly "spiritual" in the way we think of spiritual things: prophesying, teaching, exhorting, contributing, leading, doing works of mercy. But these are your spiritual worship, and they are the exercise of your gifts for the common good of the body of Christ. This all happens in view of the mercies of God. We speak because we have been spoken to by God. We teach as we are taught. We give as we have been given to. We show mercy because we have been "mercied" by God. Jesus, the high priest, offered his body on the cross as an atoning sacrifice. Christ is the victim as well as the priest. Your bodies belong to him, having been redeemed by his blood: "You were bought with a price" (1 Cor. 6:20). Being holy and acceptable in Christ, now you may "present your bodies as a living sacrifice, holy and acceptable to God. This is your spiritual worship." Free to be a living being—that is, a priest in God's holy assembly, his church.

As Sorrowful yet Always Rejoicing

A Brief Meditation on Suffering
and Joy in Paul and Luther

Stephen J. Pietsch

The title of this chapter is drawn from the well-known passage in 2 Corinthians (6:3–10) where Paul reflects on the contrasts and struggles—indeed the strange contradictions—of his life in ministry as an apostle of Christ. He says he is honored yet dishonored, slandered as well as praised, treated as an imposter even though he is genuine, as unknown yet well-known, as dying yet alive, punished yet not killed, as sorrowful yet always rejoicing, as poor but making many rich, as having nothing yet possessing everything. Paul's second letter to the Corinthians is rich in this kind of material, and it appears in plenty of other places too. You don't have to read far in Paul's letters to notice that suffering and joy are almost always found in close proximity to one another in his spiritual teaching and experience, not just as dramatic contrasts, but close partners; not merely as adjoining, but as mutually interlocking beams in Paul's ministry.

Later on in 2 Corinthians (12:10), he says: "For the sake of Christ, then, I am content with weaknesses, insults, hardships, persecutions, and calamities. For when I am weak, then I am strong." In Colossians 1 and Romans 5, he writes about rejoicing and even boasting in suffering. The modern reader may well ask: what is going on here? This is clearly more than a patient acceptance of suffering. Paul's rhetoric here takes us way beyond that. Is he disclosing to us his own heroic, apostolic love for Christ, which is so great that he is able and willing to endure all kinds of hardship? Or is this some kind of ecstatic religious masochism akin to the medieval pictures of saints being pierced and tortured as their eyes roll heavenward in spiritual rapture? And when Paul exhorts us to adopt the same attitude to suffering, what does *this* mean? What does it show us about the nature of the Christian life? What mysterious spiritual dynamic is at work here? Can *we* really be sorrowful yet always rejoicing?

Paul and His Afflictions

When we first meet Paul in the New Testament, before his dramatic conversion in Acts 9, he is of course an evil and frightening character—Saul of Tarsus, Jewish zealot, persecutor of Christ and his church. He is not suffering so much as *inflicting suffering* on Christians. In Acts 7–8, he aids and abets the execution of the deacon Stephen and then is reported to have ravaged and persecuted the church in Jerusalem, entering house after house and dragging out Christian men and women and having them thrown in prison (Acts 8:2–3).

This period in Paul's life is depicted in the film, *Paul, Apostle of Christ*. This film is an interpretation of Paul's apostolic ministry, and moreover, an interpretation of his suffering as an apostle—a theme it deals with in some depth, and in a rather imaginative way. Let me explain: Paul's complaint in 2 Corinthians 12:7–8 that he had been afflicted with a thorn in his flesh—a messenger of Satan sent to harass him—has been the topic of great speculation over the centuries. Some have suggested it was his eyesight or his digestion or some other physical malady. In the film, however, Paul's thorn in the flesh is depicted as a *mental illness*, a form of PTSD. In the film, Paul is shown waking up from nightmares and flashbacks of his evil days as a violent persecutor of Christians. He is haunted in his dreams by the faces of his victims.

What is portrayed in this film is actually a particular kind of PTSD called Moral Injury Disorder, in which people are psychologically wounded by the violence *they themselves* have inflicted on others, or participated in inflicting on others. Paul suffers agony of conscience and heart as his mind replays these horrors from his past. More than once, his character in the film wakes up in terror in a cold sweat, praying the words of 2 Corinthians 12:9: "Your grace is sufficient. Your grace is sufficient." These are the very words of God's comfort for him. This is, of course, quite consciously speculative— it's an artistic exploration. But even so, it's a rather insightful one, I would suggest.

"*Sub Contrario*" (Under the Sign of the Opposite)[1]

There is no minimizing the evil Paul did. We shouldn't downplay the suffering the young Saul of Tarsus inflicted on others. And yet, as we reflect on the transformation that followed with Paul's conversion and apostolic ministry, we see even in Paul's evil the hand of the hidden God, working *sub contrario*, bringing what Paul had intended for evil to work good and blessing. Acts 9:15–16 narrates what happens immediately after Paul's conversion on the road to Damascus. Ananias is told by God to go to Saul after his encounter with Christ in order to lay hands on him and open his eyes. This narrative is charged with almost unbearable tension and irony. Ananias is understandably terrified. He knows only too well who Saul is and is afraid he too will end up in chains if he goes to him revealing his Christian faith. We can hear in Ananias' words how astounded he is that God is sending him to *this* man of all men—this evil and dangerous man. But God answers to reassure him. This answer that God gives to Ananias is the turning point which shows the meaning and the power of Paul's whole future life—and of his future suffering in ministry. God says to Ananias: "Go, for he [Paul] is a chosen instrument of mine to carry my name before the Gentiles and kings and the children of Israel. For I will show him how much he must suffer for the sake of my name." (Acts 9:15–16).

Let's consider this. God is not merely saying "Well, Paul, you have dished out so much suffering against the church that it is now

---

[1] This Latin term, which Luther first coined in his 1518 *Heidelberg Disputation* (WA 1, 353–374), the way it is used grammatically, more accurately means "by opposite means" or "under the appearance of the opposite."

time for you to get some in return"—as punishment or as necessary chastisement. God's hand is at work much more profoundly than this, overturning human realities, redeeming human evil, transforming sinful hearts. Even as Paul intended harm to those he hurt, yet Christ—under the sign of the opposite—intends Paul to suffer in order that he may know more and more deeply, preach more and more passionately, witness more and more powerfully to God's grace, mercy, freedom and joy.

Paul's suffering for the name of Christ is the mirror image of the suffering he inflicted on Christ's church. It's an image *reversed*, an image *sub contrario*. Paul suffers not for the expiation of his sins in order to redeem himself. Christ had dealt with those sins himself once and for all. He now suffers for the sake of the gospel, for the proclamation of Christ in the world. And over the years of Paul's apostolic ministry, God's words to Ananias are fulfilled many times: he will suffer greatly for Christ's name, that name he had once reviled and persecuted.

In 2 Corinthians, chapters 4, 6, and 11, you read about this. He is flogged, imprisoned, stoned, starved, shipwrecked, humiliated. He once bound Christians in order to drag them into prison, now *he* is bound in chains and in prison in order to set others free in Christ. This is the dynamic at work in Paul's sorrowing yet always rejoicing: the gracious divine irony and severe mercy—the strange double-headed mystery of God's works—what Luther later called his "alien work" and his "proper work." What men intend for evil, God turns to good, as Joseph (Gen. 50:20) explains to his brothers who many years before had left him for dead. This is the *sub contrario* dynamic that drives Paul's rejoicing in his sufferings. And it of course all flows directly from the cross, that central fulcrum of all human history, the crucial *sub contrario* itself, which reverses the sin and death of all creation—the most horrible crime in human history transformed by God into "the greatest miracle that has ever taken place," as Luther calls it.[2]

As we look at the longer New Testament narrative of Paul's early persecution of the church, his conversion and subsequent apostolic ministry, this rhetoric of suffering and joy—which seems

---

[2] WA TR VI, 6618

strange to our modern eyes—begins to unfold and become clear. In 2 Corinthians 4:8–12, Paul says:

> We are afflicted in every way, but not crushed; perplexed, but not driven to despair; persecuted, but not forsaken; struck down, but not destroyed; always carrying in the body the death of Jesus, so that the life of Jesus may also be manifested in our bodies. For we who live are always being given over to death for Jesus' sake, so that the life of Jesus also may be manifested in our mortal flesh. So death is at work in us, but life in you.

As a young Christian reading this and similar passages (especially in 2 Cor.), they seemed to me like emotional and grandiose hyperbole. Who is this guy? I thought. What world is he living in? Little did I realize he was living in *this* world, my world, and that he was actually talking about real life in spiritually realistic terms. Little did I realize he was talking about a world that would, in time, also leave *me* perplexed and hard-pressed and struck down too. Being very young, I had not had the chance to suffer enough yet, and so I had not had the benefit of the Spirit's forging and molding that Paul describes in Romans 5:3–5: "Not only that, but we rejoice in our sufferings, knowing that suffering produces endurance, and endurance produces character, and character produces hope, and hope does not put us to shame."

Our Lives of Sorrow and Rejoicing

Here we move from considering Paul's experience of Christ's work *sub contrario* to exploring what he teaches the church about the intersection of suffering and joy in *our* lived experience with Christ Jesus. Luther, who, in some ways, walked a similar spiritual journey to Paul, strongly identifies with and testifies to this transformation through difficult experience under the hand of God. He says we must "suffer divine things."[3] Also like Paul—though contemporary

---

[3] WA 9, 97:12–14. From Luther's marginal notes on Johann Tauler's Sermons.

scholars don't say much about it—Luther knew the joy that accompanies this kind of suffering. He often observes how mysterious it is that the two live cheek-by-jowl together. In 1518, he reflected on the words of Paul in 2 Corinthians 6:10, the title of this lecture: sorrowful yet always rejoicing. He says: "In the Lord we are always to rejoice, in ourselves we are always to lament. In God we have cause to rejoice; in ourselves we have good cause for sadness. There must then be rejoicing when there is sorrow, and there will always be sorrow even as we rejoice."[4]

Here Luther picks up, with a keen experiential eye, a distinction we must take a moment to make clear. In the Christian spiritual life, as we see it lived and taught by Paul and by Luther, joy accompanies suffering. But it does not replace or supplant suffering. This is not some thinly disguised theology of glory, but a true reception of the cross. And in fact this reality is what gives Paul's rhetoric in these passages both its strangeness and its profound ring of truth. The sufferings he enumerates are not exaggerated or inflated, but carefully recorded. They are real, and they were painful and personally costly. Christians in this world will truly know agony and sorrow. As Luther says in his *Sermon on Cross and Suffering* (1530), "Very well, if I want to be Christian, I too must wear colors of the court. Our dear Lord Jesus Christ issues no other colors in his court; suffering there must be. . . . The way (of suffering) is at hand, but if you refuse to suffer, you will not become Christ's courtier."[5]

What enables us to know joy in the midst of this is that Christ is one with us in it, so that, as Luther says, we are "conformed"[6]—"cruci-formed," if you will. And so, *sub contrario*, we share completely in Christ's eternal glory, peace, joy, and freedom here and now by faith. As Paul says, echoing Jesus' own teaching, we are not like a person dying in agony, but like a woman suffering in labor—in hope of a new life (Matt. 24:8; John 16:1; Rom. 8:22). Or, as Luther memorably puts it in his *Sermon on Cross and Suffering*, with which I conclude this chapter:

---

[4] WA 1, 652:9–15. Luther is writing to his catholic opponent Prierias in regard to the Christian life, in his *Dialogue on the Power of the Pope, 1518*.

[5] WA 32, 30.

[6] WA 32, 30.

If you are willing to suffer, then the treasure and consolation which is promised and given to you is so great that you ought to suffer willingly and joyfully because Christ and his suffering are being bestowed upon you and made your own. And if you can believe this, then in time of great fear and trouble, you will be able to say: Even though I suffer long, very well then, what is that compared to that great treasure which my God has given to me—that I shall live eternally with him?[7]

---

[7] WA 32, 31.

In Statu Confessionis:
Steadfast for the Sake of Freedom

Wade R. Johnston

I was raised in Roman Catholicism. I went to a parochial school through eighth grade and then public high school. It was in my last year of high school that I became a Lutheran. At the end of that year, I was confirmed after being patiently catechized by Pastor Karl Vertz, to whom I will be forever thankful, who put up with all my questions and my objections and kept pointing me to the cross of Christ and the grace of God. When I came into Lutheranism, especially coming into American Lutheranism, I had to learn a lot of acronyms. More than acronyms, however, there was a word that I learned fairly early on that fascinated me. Lutherans, both clergy and laity, used it a lot. It was a word that I learned but didn't really understand for years. It's that kind of word. It's hard to nail down but makes more and more sense contextually with experience. Perhaps that early fascination is what led to my graduate work decades later.

The word was adiaphora. It came up often in discussions of worship or church practices. It came up when people talked about drinking, dancing, smoking, cussing, gambling, and other such things. I'd never heard the word before Lutheranism, and it seemed impossible to discuss anything within Lutheranism without it coming up. What vestments should the pastor wear? How should the church be structured? What kind of music should be played in the divine service? What type of flooring should we get when the church is remodeled? Can Bob have a beer at the church picnic? Should the school kids wear uniforms? Could the PTA do fundraisers? Should the local school have dances—and, if so, what music and what sort of dancing should be permitted?

Even more interesting, sometimes I'd hear it used as a get-out-of-jail-free card. In these situations, people didn't use it to encourage further discussion but to shut it down. It was similar to the weaker brother strategy some employ contrary to what Paul meant, where one tries to get their way by claiming offense when offense isn't really the issue (at least not biblical offense), but preferences or power. It was used to avoid providing theological rationales or coherent arguments based on sound reason and fraternal love. Even worse, sometimes it was used to justify boorish or untoward behavior.

When I began work toward a doctorate, through a number of coincidences, I ended up doing more and more work relating to the history of this word, adiaphora, and its use within the church. This research led me to the individual, perhaps more than any other, who participated in debate about both the proper meaning and abuses of this doctrine: Matthias Flacius Illyricus. I learned that debates about adiaphora weren't new and that the use of the word for less than faithful purposes wasn't either—in fact, it went back to some of the earliest days of its use in the churches of the Augsburg Confession.

Flacius' great-uncle through marriage was Baldo Lupetino, condemned to death for his evangelical views after years in prison. In spite of Protestant appeals on his behalf, he was drowned in a lagoon in Venice in September 1556. Among those interceding for Lupetino had been the princes of the Schmalkaldic League, on whose behalf Flacius had delivered a letter to Venice. Lupetino told his nephew, "*non ricantare, anzi cantare,*" "Do not recant, but sing."[1]

It was with Lupetino's encouragement that Flacius had gone north from modern-day Croatia to study theology. He studied at both Basel and Tübingen on his way to Wittenberg, making important contacts in the process. He focused especially on Hebrew and wrote a master's thesis on the contemporary debate over whether the vowel pointing in the Masoretic Text was original to the Hebrew scriptures or not. A separate paper could be written on why that debate

---

[1] Oliver K. Olson, *Matthias Flacius and the Survival of Luther's Reform* (Minneapolis: Lutheran Press, 2011), 51.

seemed so important at that time. Flacius also became very good friends with Philip Melanchthon, who looked out for him in many ways and made some important recommendations for advancing Flacius' academic career. More than Luther, Melancthon was Flacius' professional mentor.

Martin Luther profoundly influenced Flacius. While he had more contact with Melanchthon, Luther had helped him through a bout of melancholy. Luther's work, and personality, left a deep imprint on Flacius' own. Flacius primarily knew Luther in the later stages of the great reformer's life, when his writings were more polemical. Luther was for Flacius pastor, prophet, and pedagogue. Luther's Reformation, with its emphasis on pastoral care and preaching, biblical exegesis, confession, and catechesis, Flacius spent his professional life defending, with much personal sacrifice.

As the Adiaphoristic Controversy loomed on the horizon, Flacius was a Hebrew professor in Wittenberg and was, by all accounts, doing pretty well. Life seemed to be falling into place for him. At a German university, in a Protestantism dominated by northern Europeans, the Illyrian had made his way and secured a respectable position. The future looked comfortable, if not bright. Then came the death of Luther in 1546. Then 1547 brought the disastrous defeat of the Schmalkaldic League. The Holy Roman Emperor, long eager to rid his lands of heresy, now had his opportunity, his armies and allies victorious, his influence greater than ever during his lifetime in the German territories.

The Schmalkaldic League was a defensive alliance of Protestant principalities. This League, which had a fighting chance at keeping Charles V from overrunning the evangelical territories in Germany, was defeated in 1547 for several reasons. Most notable among them was the betrayal of Moritz, Duke of Saxony (Albertine Saxony), the cousin of the Elector of Saxony (Ernestine Saxony). Moritz, while a Lutheran, teamed up with the emperor to gain territory and the electoral title from John Frederick. This caused the League to fight on multiple fronts, which is never an easy task. At long last, undistracted by other threats, Charles V finally had the opportunity to address the Protestant problem in Germany, and he was determined to make the most of it.

The electoral title was a big deal. Moritz had reason to covet it. The elector was one of the few people, seven in total, who got to elect the emperor. That a duke would desire to expand his lands is also hardly surprising (his territorial gains included Wittenberg when all was said and done). Moritz was a Lutheran and was not abandoning his faith, at least not in his own mind. These were political calculations. How he expected Lutheranism to survive is uncertain, but he did not seem to think that he couldn't be both a Lutheran and ally of the emperor, at least for the time being. However, the defeat of John Frederick threw Lutheranism into disarray and made Moritz an extremely unpopular figure, even among his subjects. He became known as the Judas of Meissen. While he had increased his power, his grip on it was tenuous. Nervous evangelicals looked to Wittenberg, yet just as its voice was desperately needed, it found itself under a new ruler. Almost immediately after securing his new title and lands, he began plotting how he could work against the emperor and solidify his gains.

Charles V was now determined to pursue a re-catholicizing agenda. His approach was gradual. He began with a focus on practice and some compromise formulae on areas of doctrinal disagreement. He wanted his counter-reform to bring long-lasting success. He recognized that wasn't possible with heavy-handed and extremely unpopular measures attacking central issues right out of the gates. The product of this concern was the *Augsburg Interim*, the new imperial religious policy for Germany. Some Lutheran territories had retained some of the practices mandated in this *Interim*. Others had long done away with them. Either way, the state was now requiring them. The emperor, who wanted to restore the jurisdiction of Roman bishops, was himself taking on an ecclesiastical role. The Roman Church, which would never have warmly welcomed such intervention in territories under its control, was willing to accept such state action in this instance.

The *Augsburg Interim* was initially most influential in the more southern German territories, where imperial troops had more of a presence. It would take longer for it to be enforced in the north, but persecution increased. As they were able, authorities allied with the emperor reintroduced the canon of the mass, episcopal ordination, and the seven sacraments. Lutherans still got some things like

communion in both kinds, but the temporary nature of such con-
cessions wasn't hard to predict. The reintroduction of the jurisdiction of bishops, in essence, meant the reintroduction of the papacy.
The gradualism of this approach was merely tactical. There was no
intention for long-term compromise. Already the doctrine on which
the church stands or falls was undermined with a very problematic
compromise formula on justification.

Phillip Melanchthon, who later became a bitter opponent
when Flacius rejected his moderating approach to state coercion
in religious affairs, opposed the *Augsburg Interim*, even under the
new elector, who had defeated and unseated his former prince. He
thought too much was being given up. He was vocal in his opposition
to the new religious policy. This was not an easy stand to take, but
Melanchthon stood firm. Confessional Lutherans sometimes forget
how much Melanchthon sacrificed and gave up for the Reformation.
While Melanchthon wavered and compromised in the Adiaphoristic
Controversy with and following the Leipzig Interim, he was hardly
a coward. He was a man who gave much for the sake of the gospel.

Nicolaus von Amsdorf, another longtime friend and colleague
of Luther's, part of his inner circle, also spoke out loudly against the
Augsburg Interim. Amsdorf had been a key player in the Reformation
taking hold in Magdeburg, which would be the site of Lutheranism's
last stand, at least in the eyes of the Gnesio-Lutherans, who opposed
the interims. Magdeburg fairly early on became a hotspot of resistance to Charles V's re-catholicizing agenda within Germany. Flacius
would later, somewhat reluctantly, find his way there to help fight the
resistance and fuel it with pamphlets. Together, the pastors and theologians gathered in the city articulated a clear and detailed confession
of what it was to be a true heir of Luther's reform and the Word of
God in such trying times.

The *Augsburg Interim* was despised in Moritz's lands and among
Lutherans elsewhere. Increasingly, he was viewed as an enemy of
his own confession. The more vocally Magdeburg and others spoke
out, the worse it was for Moritz's standing and stability in his realm.
He realized that if they pushed too hard on the new religious policy,
there would be a backlash he might not weather well. As noted earlier,
he also seems to have always intended to remain a Lutheran, and he
likely became increasingly aware that the future of his confession

was increasingly bleak. He could not have his cake and eat it too. More and more, it appeared he could either side with the emperor for the long term or remain a Lutheran. The *Augsburg Interim* was too much. Moritz and others like him were the frogs in the water whose temperature was slowly being raised. Moritz turned to his newly acquired Wittenberg theologians for help. He wanted a better proposal, something with compromise formulae that would keep the emperor happy but retain as much as possible of Lutheran doctrine and practice. Beyond the emperor, he wanted to placate his subjects and coreligionists as well.

The Wittenberg theologians set upon the task, putting together the *Leipzig Proposal*, labeled the Leipzig Interim by its opponents. This is where the term "adiaphora" becomes very important. An *adiaphoron*, singular, is something that is neither commanded nor forbidden in scripture. More than that, it's something that is supposed to be a middle thing—it's supposed to be indifferent. It doesn't bring a lot of baggage with it. It can serve for edification, but it's not necessary one way or another. It can be useful. For example, the gospel can be preached whether I stand at a pulpit with a microphone or not, but a pulpit and microphone can be very helpful for the preaching of the gospel. Adiaphora can come to represent important concepts as well. A pulpit reminds people of the importance of the preached word. It's where people come to expect the good news to sound—this is a good thing. Some adiaphora can involve things near and dear to people's hearts.

Moritz's territory had not gone undergone as much liturgical reform as some other places in Germany. It still retained some of the liturgical trappings and practices eliminated elsewhere. Some things, therefore, that seemed acceptable compromises in Moritz's lands came across as big impositions in other Protestant areas. An example would be what we today call the surplice. A simple vestment, most Lutherans today would hardly bat an eye at a pastor wearing one. This was not the case in the Adiaphoristic Controversy. This vestment took on enormous significance. Flacius would insist that the devil was behind the surplice. Mandating the re-establishment of such things raised serious questions, especially under state coercion.

Questions about adiaphora, or supposed adiaphora, gave rise to Lutheranism's first major identity crisis, and a host of other debates would flow from it. Things purportedly indifferent led to disputes about doctrine at the very core of Luther's Reformation. Multiple attacks on the gospel arose from this controversy, not merely from without but from within Lutheranism. Fault lines long present were now exposed. What Charles V would not be able to do—destroy the evangelical movement—the evangelicals themselves might do, it appeared. Even in this *Leipzig Proposal*, which was supposed to limit the damage to the evangelical cause, the statement on justification was ambiguous at best. Flacius and others, perplexed by the willingness of their former colleagues and mentors to yield so much, saw no other route but fierce resistance. They set out against the Leipzig Interim with everything at their disposal, primarily the printing press.

Flacius went to work. His pace was astonishing, his pen furiously turning out arguments against the interims. He wrote at first under pseudonyms. Some hid his identity better than others. The aliases were probably meant more to avoid readers dismissing his arguments than to conceal his identity for personal reasons. Flacius always admitted that his German was not as polished as he would have liked. He wished others would take up the cause and take over his work. He felt compelled, however, to defend the gospel that had brought him north to Germany. Mocked as a foreigner, even by the normally irenic Melanchthon, he knew that his voice did not carry the same weight as a German's would have.

Nevertheless, he was successful. His labeling of the *Leipzig Proposal* as the Leipzig Interim stuck, which would fatally wound his relationship with Melanchthon, who considered Flacius unfair and too polemical in his criticisms. His pamphlets proved convincing to many. His writing was accessible to laity and clergy alike. He avoided wordiness (according to the standards of his time) and kept key themes prominent. He had a knack for coining phrases and using memorable imagery.

The sense of betrayal between Flacius and Melanchthon was reciprocal, as was the case between many key figures in the debates that broke out now and in subsequent years. Flacius might not have meant to leave Wittenberg permanently when he first departed, but this was an irreparable break. His Magdeburg years were perhaps his most peaceful, sadly. After his Jena years, he became a pilgrim for

much of the rest of his life, a reward for his faithfulness in Magdeburg.
The cross marked his life, though perhaps not his grave.

Flacius took great pains to define true adiaphora as part of his
struggle against false adiaphora. In *A Book about True and False
Adiaphora,* he explains:

> One should now observe that there are three grounds for establishing
> adiaphora. The first is the general command of God that he wants to
> have everything in the church done in an orderly and proper fashion
> and to serve for edification, inasmuch as he is a God of order and not
> of disorder. The second is the free Christian desire of the church. . . .
> The third are the judicious, God-fearing people for whom the church
> is inclined to establish such adiaphora. This is what may be said about
> the establishment of adiaphora.[2]

Adiaphora should serve for the good of the people and have a
rationale behind them. This is crucial. There should be a "why" that
those introducing a practice can explain. One could have argued the
"adiaphora" in the *Leipzig Proposal* were for good order for peace,
but they didn't flow from the free consent of the church. They also
weren't crafted to benefit the people they were meant to serve, but
rather they were intended to placate enemies who were making very
serious threats.

Another important difference was that Melanchthon saw a clear
distinction between doctrine and practice, where Flacius and the other
Magdeburg theologians did not. Melanchthon thought some aspects
of church practice (and perhaps even teaching) could be placed under
the state's control (for instance, while the state shouldn't mandate
piety, it could prohibit certain foods on certain days or set aside certain days for special observances). Here, too, the Magdeburg theologians objected. The church, not the state, was responsible for what it
taught and what it practiced. The state had no business coercing what
belonged to the church's jurisdiction and free consent: that which
defined, informed, or influenced faith. What we do flows from what
we believe. The church is called to preach, catechize, and carry out
its work in good order (how it organizes itself, how the divine service

---

[2] Flacius, *Ein buch, von waren und falschen Mitteldingen,* Jiii v.

is structured and celebrated, etc.). When confession is necessary in a time of controversy, practice takes on immense importance because what we do can undermine the faith. Bad practice can, especially in such a time, cloud and weaken true doctrine. There could probably be no worse time for the state to interfere.

For Flacius, ceremonies served as sermons for the eyes. They could catechize or lead astray. This was especially true in a less literate age. Many Christians know this. It is no small thing when changes are made regarding what happens on Sunday. People notice. People care, and for good reason. While adiaphora are indifferent things, what we do with them, and what they act in the service of, are not.

Magdeburg insisted that nothing is an adiaphoron in a time of controversy; when coercion is involved, offense is given, and a clear confession is necessary. The Formula of Concord would later agree, vindicating their position. The Magdeburg printing presses ran unremittingly. Not since Luther had so much been produced by the printing press at such a pace. Many of their pamphlets were thrown over the wall and disseminated to those occupying the territories around them, asking German troops, "Why are you going to attack your fellow Germans?" and asking fellow evangelicals who found themselves in armies allied with the emperor, "Why are you going to attack fellow Protestants?" Publications were smuggled abroad as well, drawing attention to the city's plight on account of its faithfulness to God's Word and good order.

Finally, the siege ended. Neither party could claim military victory, but Magdeburg's confession still stood. Luther's gospel still sounded. His Reformation lived on. Moritz and some of the other Germans then turned on the emperor, and his forces were pushed back. And yet, while the territories in which Lutherans lived had the relief of greater political peace, this was only the beginning of doctrinal controversies that would continue for decades until the *Formula of Concord*.

Adiaphora still provide plenty of opportunities for divisions to reveal themselves and multiply today. Practice and doctrine, as then, still belong together, yet many strive to separate them or place parts of one or another outside of the church's jurisdiction and free consent. Free things are still in places treated as law. Love often takes a backseat to preferences or frivolity. There is still a lack of rationale behind much of what the church does, whether in introducing change or reintroducing old practices. Indifferent things still matter. People can still use them to rob us of Christian freedom or abuse our glorious liberty through a lack of love.

The church must always make decisions. Doctrine must be taught and applied in the times we live, in the languages we speak, in the spaces in which we find ourselves. Practices must fit the same. While hopefully we are spared times like those Flacius and Melanchthon and their contemporaries faced, adiaphora remains, and we must navigate our own time well. The gospel deserves our best. Our hearers need to be able to see and hear clearly of Christ's love to them. The church must protect Christian freedom and cultivate Christian love. At the risk of being annoyingly repetitive, indifferent things matter. Galatians 5 is still a great model for our life together in Christ. Paul urges us, "It is for freedom that Christ has set us free. Stand firm, then, and do not let yourselves be burdened again by a yoke of slavery" (Gal. 5:1). And Paul reminds us, "The only thing that counts is faith expressing itself through love" (Gal. 5:6b).

One of my favorite observations about adiaphora came from my church body's president, Wisconsin Evangelical Lutheran Synod President Mark Schroeder. I can't remember if this was in a paper or if he was speaking off-the-cuff, but he said it at a pastor's conference I attended. He said, "When we have established something is an adiaphoron, it's not where the conversation ends, it's where it begins." I think that's a very helpful thing for us to remember, as we seek to be loving brothers and sisters in the church. When we establish something is an adiaphoron, then we can discuss the why? Why would we want to do it? How will it help edify? How will it serve the gospel in the church's mission? We can begin to weed out those things that are, as our confessions say, simply frivolities—those things being introduced without proper justification or process, those things that might water down our confession or confuse the difference between our message and the message of less orthodox, evangelical confessions. Then we can seek to find practices that are conducive to our doctrine, that amplify the gospel, that keep Christ at the center, helping people to gladly hear and learn God's Word without distraction, and helping visitors understand what matters most to us because it matters most to God.

As Christians, we are free. Christian freedom is no cheap thing. It cost the very blood of God. We should cherish it, protect it, and exercise it. As Christians, we love as Christ. We are God's gifts to our neighbor, channels of his love, masks of God. Christian freedom without Christian love is an excuse for sin and no freedom at all, but a return to slavery. Christian love without Christian freedom is no love at all but a return to a transactional relationship with either God or neighbor, or both. Times change, but the Christian life doesn't. We live freely, in love. Those who strove against the interims did that, for their brothers and sisters in Christ, and those not yet in him, and for us yet to be born. May we do the same, in freedom and love.

Fanatic Iconoclasts
are Stupid and Dangerous:
Luther's *Invocavit* Sermons

Steven D. Paulson

If you didn't know it before the pandemic, now you have proof that bondage of the will does not end well for humans. We don't like it, and so we rebel. We hated the lockdowns and the confinement to quarters. By imposition of state power, don't go anywhere, don't work, don't travel, don't socialize! Wear a mask! In "social distancing" we even have a word for this new monasticism. One of the causes of the lockdown and its worldly monasticism is supposedly also its cure—which in theology we call *fanaticism*. Fanaticism arises from both an uncontrollable fear of death, as well as a Messianic complex that leads people to think certain individuals (doctors, politicians, religious figures) will save them. Religions routinely get fanatical preachers, but so do secular societies—perhaps especially secular ones. The first sign of fanaticism is hysteria over death and warnings of the coming apocalypse. Fanatics always tell you that they have had a baptism of the Holy Spirit. And of this Spirit, they themselves are the prophet and spokesman. The second sign of fanaticism is rebellion over being bound. You know you're dealing with fanatics when you have hordes and mobs that refuse to be locked down, imprisoned, and confined. Freedom at any cost is the slogan of this kind of fanaticism.

We must take notice, as Luther did in his day, that fanaticism is not only the devil's attack—but is a special kind of satanic activity.

Luther calls it a "flank" attack because it comes unexpectedly. This kind of attack is always the deadliest. The devil makes it appear as if he were using the law to bring a righteous cause into effect. He appears as an agent of justice in society by tearing down the old law and asserting a new and better one. That's why the attack is unexpected. It comes as a proposition for a better law than the one we already have. Lutherans have to speak up as the voices of both salvation and reason in the face of two things: (1) our attempts to use the law to save ourselves and (2) the rebellion against the law that happens when it's clear that it can't save.

The only thing the world knows, after all, is the law. And if locking you down won't save you, then neither will getting rid of the law. The law of nations has its place—which only the Christian, having been freed from the law, can understand. When Paul tells us to obey the government, he's not merely capitulating to Roman colonialism. He understands the place of the law in this old world. But there is also a place the law doesn't belong, and that's in the conscience. The law is not your savior, nor did it ever make anyone free. It can't give eternal life or provide an escape from death. The law was never given to us creatures for such purposes. Only Jesus Christ saves—through a word that is the opposite of the law. But what could such a word be? The word of Jesus Christ is not nihilism, anarchy, or lawlessness (like the world thinks), but is the gospel. Christ's word is the forgiveness of sin and therefore the end of the law (Gal. 3:25).

Iconoclasts

Iconoclasm is one of the first and most apparent signs of the theological disease that Luther called *fanaticism*. Luther himself had to deal with it many times. Whenever one fanatic was put down, another arose. And so Luther referred to them as *Schwermerei*—those who buzz like bees. That was Luther's term for the mob mentality that always comes with fanaticism. By this point, Luther was a public enemy of the state and the church. After the Diet of Worms (1521), Prince Frederick the Wise had him kidnapped and secured in Wartburg Castle for Luther's own safety. Meanwhile, the Reformation continued in Wittenberg without Luther. While Luther was locked up, his friend Andreas Bodenstein von Karlstadt decided to ignite a rebellion—as all good fanatics do. Except in this case, it was directed against Luther himself. Karlstadt began preaching about purifying the churches. The foolish ones who listened to him—the mob—began destroying images and altars and forcing communion in both kinds on the people. They had been oppressed for years by saints they could not imitate, and they weren't going to take it anymore.

The real problem with Karlstadt is that he taught direct, unmediated, inner illumination of the Spirit. This is an old pagan, Platonic theory which claims that preaching and teaching are unnecessary if the Spirit falls upon you miraculously. Whether you're a dirt farmer or a scholar at the university, you have the truth inside—and now need only to force the external world to fit this internal revelation. Such inner revelation is always a revelation of the law and therefore ascribes to itself the authority to reform the old world into God's preferred political order. Likewise, the Zwickau prophets Storch, Drechsel, and Stübner—who were all tied in with Thomas Müntzer—rejected infant baptism and rid themselves of Christ's incarnate body in the Lord's Supper by turning it into a mere sign. Then, they tore down altars and statues of saints and set forth a new, "corrected" liturgy. They even went about imposing a new world order based on what they thought was the basic principle of God's law: equality for all, which meant economic and political equality of the working peasants.

Melanchthon was not much help as a leader at this point—he couldn't quite figure the difference between law and gospel in such circumstances. And so Luther finally came out of isolation into the midst of the mob, delivering some of his most famous sermons: the eight *Invocavit* sermons. Luther had two goals for his preaching at this time. The first was to restore order in society, which is where the law really belongs. Because fanatics can't tell the difference between law and gospel, iconoclasm and the forcible imposition of false justice must be stopped. Second, Luther wanted to free Christians into the gospel, because only in the gospel does the law come to an end. This is an external word rather than an internal revelation, and so the law comes to an end in Christ incarnate and preached. To understand how Luther dealt with fanaticism, it is important to note his clearest discussion about enthusiasm in the *Smalcald Articles*.

Luther found that enthusiasm and fanaticism are not just periodic problems, but that they are the form of original sin itself. This is to say that the original sin is refusing to seek God where he wants to be found and instead trying to find him where sinners always go—that is, inside themselves. Luther trots out two main figures to illustrate this: Müntzer, who led the peasants' revolt into terrible slaughter, and the Pope, who made the mass into an act of a sacrifice rather than a promise preached. Both kinds of fanatics sought God "within"—which is the meaning of the word *enthusiasm.* They believed that they had a Spirit who had given them power to bring in the kingdom of God on earth and save humanity from destruction.

The marks of this fanatical pattern are clear. Fanaticism involves the rejection of the local preacher in favor of a heroic, spirit-filled, charismatic individual. But it also involves violent rebellion against government as the way to establish peace and justice. Icons are either worshipped or destroyed, depending on whether the fanatic wants direct mediation of God or desires to keep God and creation separate. Finally, the fanatic always rejects the presence of Christ in earthly things—and in the sacraments, above all. Fanatics always destroy the sacraments by seeking an absent Christ, and so they reject the power of baptism for infants and the body and blood of Christ in the Supper, and they destroy absolution, whether it is public or private. With these features of fanaticism in mind, we can turn now to the sermons Luther preached over the course of a week in Wittenberg.

Luther's First Sermon

This first *Invocavit* sermon begins with stunning words: "The summons of death comes to us all, and no one can die for another. Everyone must fight his own battle with death by himself, alone. . . . You can't shout into another's ears."[1] The mob can't compel the individual when it comes to what ultimately matters in life—like death and the final judgment. This is very hard for modern people to grasp, since the main part of being modern is to accept the Darwinian idea that it is not the individual that matters, but the collective. Only the

---

[1] LW 51:70.

species survives—not any one individual. While that is very true in the old world, it is not what Jesus Christ brings.

Mobs, rebellion, and fanaticism begin with a premise: it is not about the individual, but the group—not the one, but the many. You get your identity from the group, not from yourself. This theory infects fanaticism of all kinds, but especially the modern forms that say justification cannot be individual. Justice involves the species, the group, the community, and the collective. Today we call this *identity*—that which makes you identifiable from others is the group that you belong to. Today this is called "identity politics," and it finds its origins with philosophers like Hegel and Darwin's evolutionary theory. Lone pushback to this preference for the collective came from that odd Dane, Søren Kierkegaard, with his contention that "truth is subjectivity"—it's not a matter of the group. The problems with Kierkegaard are many, but he did see the first problem with fanaticism.

Luther's position is the opposite of all identity politics: You are alone in your battle with death! The final judgment is the only thing that really counts, and you stand before it alone. You can't get more individual than that. God doesn't judge by category or group, but for fanatics, everything revolves around which group you're in. Thus, even the nature of your birth as male or female can be changed. Sexuality as a social product is set forth as true freedom, which doesn't depend on the genitalia you were born with, but which group you want to identify with. Luther has none of that. God's judgment is not about Jew or Gentile, slave or free, male or female. In death, you're all alone, standing there naked before God with the stuff you were born with—not as a race or a sexual identity, but as yourself.

Therefore, Luther first says that you must "know you are children of wrath" (Eph. 2:3). You are not children either of privilege or of victimhood. Original sin is not that you were born into poverty and tried to get out, or that you were born rich and tried to give it away. Original sin means that you have no preacher and do not trust God because you had no promise from him. You stood there under his wrath. That wrath is the law's only outcome. The law doesn't end in history's long arc of justice or as a reward for doing the right thing. The law ends only in God's wrath, which is God's intense, total, and eternal hatred of you.

Now, if that's all you knew—poor you! It would indeed be better to identify with a group and hope for the best. But that's not all God has to say. He has a second word: God has sent his only begotten Son. To lead the mob into revolution to purify the church and bring justice in the world? No, it is to be free from sin as a child of God. And how do you get free? By destroying your master in a coup? By refusing to be enslaved? By fighting powerlessness by becoming empowered? No, you are freed from sin, death, and God's wrath only by faith in God's word. But to believe in the name of Jesus Christ, someone had to give it to you first. You get God from the outside in an external word. This word is not the law, but a simple promise of *I forgive you.* Suddenly, without effort, and without the law, God makes you no longer a child of wrath, but a child of God (Jn. 1:12).

Following faith comes love. Yet, this does not mean that love is the thing that really saves rather than faith—that's the position of a fanatic. Fanatics think that love is the measure of God's judgment in the end. But an evangelical—who isn't a fanatic—knows that faith is everything. Faith is not a starting point, but is life's destination—and only so does faith justify without the law. Yet faith now creates love in the way a tree produces fruit—naturally, automatically, without knowledge or will. Neither knowledge nor will ever produces much love at all. In fact, they produce hate while touting themselves as factories of love. Luther knew that you can't love by attempting to do it. Even the great Golden Rule understands that self-love can't quite deliver. You'll never create love by trying to love a group, an idea, an abstraction, or a species.

So, Luther says, you don't get love from loving the group you identify with. You get love from believing Christ's promise—not by finding the best in others or loving people by correcting the errors of morality they can't see because of their own privilege or power. You get love when you are thankful for all God's gifts—and especially the word of forgiveness, which is the chief of them. The gospel isn't a system or a process in which words function according to the law. The gospel preached is something organic, which is to say that it works without thinking, proposing, or willing. The gospel works organically because it is the nature of the plant to bear its fruit apart from effort or striving.

Love is also not a matter of mouthing doctrines. Luther saw how this happened in Wittenberg, since fanatics actually love doctrine. They love slogans that can be placarded in protest. Though the Wittenbergers complained of their poverty and oppression, worst of all to Luther was that they could mouth the doctrine of justification by faith alone. They knew the slogan, but couldn't preach it—let alone hear it. In this case, justification becomes just another formula. It's a mere token of being part of a social group, even if that group is named Lutheran. But the gospel is no slogan. It is the particular practice of faith that preaches this word in baptism, the Lord's Supper, and the absolution. Only in this external word is justification by faith alone to be found.

For all that, there is something else that faith produces along with love. The highest form of love, Luther says, is "patience"[2]— which is something the fanatics don't have. They demand change, rights, power, and all their freedoms right now! How much longer must I wait for my part of the pie? And so fanatics try to take what's theirs by force. Impatience is a chief sign of fanaticism because it cannot deal with churches or politics moving slowly toward change. Fanatics are impatient because they know nothing of the gospel; they only know the law, which is not patient, but demands deeds right now. Law demands full, total, complete, present righteousness. It cannot stand any injustice, especially against itself, because the law has no patience for imperfection.

The iconoclasts had no patience with imperfection either. So they tore down statues in churches and followed Karlstadt's insistence on immediate imposition of proper communion practice. They knew nothing about patience, since patience involves persecution and suffering, which fanatics don't tolerate. Therefore, Luther observes, the main sign of love is not that you have changed society for the good of a dispossessed group—like Müntzer would later do with the peasants in Switzerland—but that you yourself suffer persecution. Patience comes when you recognize inequality and thus learn patience with weakness.

Yet the gospel must be preached and published openly—the church isn't for anything else. Luther was hard as nails on the public

---

[2] LW 51:71.

preaching of the gospel, despite whatever offended consciences it produced.[3] When the gospel was preached in Wittenberg, it immediately raised important questions about the canon of the mass, which supposed that the Lord's Supper was a sacrifice offered to God in appeasement of his wrath. Karlstadt's solution for the problem of the eucharistic prayer was to cancel the mass entirely. But this was not Luther's way. The mass can't be cancelled in disregard for good order, which is much of what liturgy is about—to say nothing of politics.

Luther did understand that the mass was evil. The eucharistic prayer, as it's called, put sacrifice at the center of the liturgy as either appeasement of God or a fantasy of participation in the eternal law. Luther wouldn't have any of it, and he had by this point removed the eucharistic prayer entirely—consecrating the bread and wine with Christ's words of institution alone. But even in 1522, Luther said that if the canon of mass weren't so evil, he would reintroduce it after Karlstadt's impatient surgery of the liturgy. Though the fanatics have dismembered the mass, reform must continue by restoring the elements of worship: liturgy, sacraments, and preaching of the gospel. Luther even tells the churches that they could have written to him in the Wartburg Castle, yet he received no such inquiry, nor was he asked about how to properly conduct the Lord's Supper.

But fanatics don't operate this way, claiming instead to have the Holy Spirit moving within them. And by this false moving of the Spirit, they are deceived by charismatic leaders. Indeed, Karlstadt claimed that he abolished the mass at the prompting of the Spirit within him. But Luther replies: "Here one can see that you do not have the Spirit, even though you have a deep knowledge of the Scriptures."[4] The work of the Spirit is not something secret, drumming up new things no one's ever heard of before. This is why it's easy to know if you have the Holy Spirit or an evil spirit: the one produces the preaching of the gospel, but the other produces mob rule.

Luther notes a few other things that fanatics don't understand. One of these is that fanatics don't grasp what it means to stand firm in faith. With faith, only one thing is necessary, namely, faith in the promise. This isn't a belief like any other, but is faith that Christ alone

---

[3] LW 51:73.
[4] LW 51:74.

makes you righteous before the eternal throne of God at Judgment Day. What this means for the church is that liturgy and sacraments have only one necessary component, which is that they give the simple word of forgiveness. This word is delivered in baptism, the Lord's Supper, the generous outpouring of sermons, and the absolution— both public and private. Fanatics fixate on imposing rules: whether it's both elements of bread and wine in the mass or meeting the demands of the peasants. But they lose the one thing necessary in the process, which is that the gospel must be preached. This turns the gospel into its opposite, making the law the measurement that determines if one is a Christian or not.

If fanatics misunderstand what is necessary concerning faith, they also lose true Christian freedom. To the fanatics, freedom means being part of an identity group—whether it's the evangelicals of Wittenberg or the peasants with Müntzer. But when it comes to Christians, freedom doesn't mean belonging to a certain group. Freedom belongs to love, and love belongs to the neighbor. The necessity of faith is the promise of the gospel given to you apart from free will, which means that Christ isn't waiting for you to make a decision or accept his offer. His promise isn't posed as a question. Before the promise of the gospel, there is no free will. But once the promise of Jesus Christ removes free will, you have true and utter freedom—not only in the final judgment, but here and now before the neighbor. Fanatics can't stand this kind of freedom; they want to be the ones who decide what the neighbor needs, and then impose the consequences on you. They deem themselves experts about what the group *really* needs. But Luther rejects any such attempt to remove the gospel's freedom.

Luther's Second Sermon

In his second sermon, Luther proceeds to note another aspect of the fanaticism at work in Wittenberg with Karlstad's forced changes to the mass. Luther recognized that, as the original reformer, he had to take account of how the mob mentality works. You can get people caught up in a mob regarding communion services or how to help the poor people of the city get food. But Luther recognized what the fanatics don't, which is that you must first win the hearts of the people. They shouldn't be forced simply by the will of the majority. Further than this, the gospel is not like politics, which must rely on the persuasion of free wills. The gospel doesn't persuade, but wins hearts differently than fiery or flowery rhetoric. The gospel wins the hearts of individuals instead of groups. The church doesn't operate the way politics does because hearts are won by giving a promise rather than persuading a free will.

In other words, fanatics think that the word of God is a general rule or law. Karlstadt thought God was telling him by some inner spirit the right thing to do with the mass. His followers did as he said; otherwise they would be cut off. But the word of God is both law and gospel. So Luther says in his second sermon that "Faith must not be chained and imprisoned nor bound by an ordinance to any work."[5] Fanatics always try to bind faith to works, because the fanatic always supposes that he knows what the Holy Spirit really wants. So while Karlstadt tried to use political power to change the mass, Luther arrives and refuses to use politics to get what he wants. Instead, he preaches.

And, in this way, Luther's preaching isn't like political speech-making. All changes in church that help the neighbor must come through the power of the word of promise. When the promise is given, change will come freely instead of by force. It's at this point that Luther delivers one of his most famous lines: "I simply taught, preached and wrote God's Word; otherwise I did nothing. And while I slept, or drank Wittenberg beer with my friends Philip and Amsdorf, the Word so greatly weakened the papacy that no prince or emperor ever inflicted such losses upon it. I did nothing; the Word did everything."[6] Just so, Luther quotes Psalm 33:6: "The Lord made heaven (and earth) by the word!" So, Luther says, contrary to fanatics: "we spread the Word alone."[7] Luther refuses to appeal to the mob, instead leaving the question of both kinds in the sacrament up to the individual. As with Paul and circumcision, it is immaterial whether to keep it or not, because the real problem is the attempt to get freedom out

---

[5] LW 51:77.
[6] LW 51:77.
[7] LW 51:78.

of the law. As Luther notes, wherever you make one law, a thousand more come right behind it. Therefore, you cannot mandate freedom.[8]

Luther's Third Sermon

Then, in the third sermon, Luther took up the matter of icons, and so also the first commandment. One of the consistent features of fanatics is that they are terribly bothered by images of God, the gods, or heroes. There is a reason for this: images at their foundation disobey the first and most basic commandment, they say. In brief, images seem to force you to worship ancestors—the heroes and saints of the past. This worship destroys the basis for fanaticism, which is that we shouldn't follow the rules of the past. The fanatic asserts himself against the past in order to give new and improved laws that will sanctify both the fanatic and the broader society in need of change. The fanatic imagines that he—not the ancestors—has the true law by which God will bring in his new utopian kingdom.

When you don't know the gospel and its freedom, you have to use the law as salvation because it's all you have. But this maneuver has a consistent and costly result: it breaks society, politics, and the church into camps. On the one side are those who worship the law of the ancestors and their traditions. They hold to the past and its wisdom. Today, we usually call this camp conservative. On the other side are the fanatics who say that God is now showing new and unheard of things by a charismatic working of the Spirit. They find in this revelation a new form of justice that will free those held under the old laws and empower them. Fanatics hold that the law must be revised completely to lift up the impoverished and enslaved. Equality and empowerment are the chosen methods of this camp. But what you end up with is not freedom but a new "Spirit-law," which teaches how to organize society around fairness, equality, and empowerment. Spirit-law, the fanatics suppose, will sanctify and justify the world. And so the fanatics take down the old images and build new, improved, Spirit-filled ones. If they go far enough, as the Muslims have, they forbid any and all images of heroes or God. To be pure is

---

[8] LW 51:78.

to have no icons—and thus immediate contact with the unpreached God and his eternal law.

Luther is commonly associated with one of these two groups, either conservative or radical—guided either by the law of the ancestors or the new and improved Spirit-law. But in fact, he belongs to neither camp, and is probably one of very few who doesn't. Luther sums up his argument against Karlstadt by saying that we must not confuse matters of freedom with the one necessary thing of faith. Liberty is not a law that can be enforced by imposition. Therefore, images, statues, and paintings are all matters of freedom. That also makes them neither necessary nor unnecessary for faith. Karlstadt, like all fanatics since, tried to use Exodus 20:4 and the older, rabbinic way of reading the first commandment: "You shall not make for yourself a carved image, or any likeness of anything that is in heaven above, or that is in the earth beneath, or that is in the water under the earth." On this passage the fanatics take their stand against icons.[9]

Yet the fanatics try to make a distinction between "making" an image—which may be all right—and "worshiping" an image, even though the text clearly prohibits "making" any image. But then we have all the patriarchs making altars, God commanding two birds to be erected on the mercy seat (Ex. 37:7), and, best of all, Moses commanding his people to erect a bronze serpent to which the poisoned must look in order to be saved (Num. 21:9).[10] In spite of these Old Testament examples, the iconoclasts in Wittenberg decided to destroy altars and images and impose their righteous cause on everyone else. But this is not Luther's way: reform does not consist in chopping down statues or destroying altars, but in preaching the word alone. Luther says that they should have preached that "images [are] nothing and that no service is done to God by erecting them."[11] Let the proclamation of the gospel do the work of reform and leave matters of worship to the realm of freedom.

Luther also knew that this fanatic iconoclasm toward purity by law always has a backlash; not only does it fail to get rid of the idols, but it actually makes people cling to them more than ever. Fanatics

---

[9] LW 51:82.
[10] LW 51:82.
[11] LW 51:83.

destroy altars, only for many more to be set up in defiance of their impositions. Luther's solution to this is to magnify the work of ministry (*ministerium*) instead of its effect (*executio*).[12] The point is that the preacher should attend to the preaching of the word alone, rather than fixate on whatever political effect he wants to get out of it. Thus, true freedom consists in two things: (1) complete trust in the word to do what it says, and (2) patience for the time being, since freedom cannot be imposed by force.[13]

There is therefore the one and only "must" for Christians: that this gospel word go out wherever the Lord wants it. Preach and teach, and then let the word do its work of reform. Fanatics reject this external word and therefore also the power of the gospel. They confuse the Holy Spirit with their supposedly new law, because the law is the only thing fanatics know. The Holy Spirit doesn't conform to fanatical dreams of utopia, because the Spirit puts himself in a definite place through the instruments of the holy ministry: the preaching of the gospel and the giving of the sacraments. Consequently, fanatics destroy the sacraments themselves—beginning with baptism and proceeding to the Lord's Supper and absolution. They reconstruct the church and the world according to their vision of whatever new law supposedly makes people holy. Then they cut, cancel, force, and destroy their way into condemning the only thing that saves sinners, produces love, and makes true good works: the word that comes not from within, but through a simple preacher declaring the one word Jesus gave us to say: "I forgive you all of your sin."

---

[12] LW 51:83.
[13] LW 51:91.

www.ingramcontent.com/pod-product-compliance
Lightning Source LLC
Chambersburg PA
CBHW022013080426

42733CB00007B/587